Seven Declarations for an

unshakable life

Embracing Every Day with Passion and Confidence

FRANK DAMAZIO

PUBLISHED BY CITY CHRISTIAN PUBLISHING
9200 NE Fremont, Portland, Oregon 97220

City Christian Publishing is a ministry of City Bible Church and is dedicated to serving the local church and its leaders through the production and distribution of quality equipping resources. It is our prayer that these materials, proven in the context of the local church, will equip leaders in exalting the Lord and extending His kingdom.

For a free catalog of additional resources from City Christian Publishing, please call 1-800-777-6057 or visit our web site at www.CityChristianPublishing.com.

First Edition, January 2007
Printed in the United States of America

Contents

Dedication

I dedicate this book to my dear friend Wendell Smith who pastors the City Church of Seattle. For over thirty years he has lived out and modeled these unshakable declarations in all seasons of life. He has lived strong, held his head high, turned to God at all times and has never lost heart. May his spirit of faith be reproduced in all who seek to live the unshakable life.

Introduction

Seven Declarations for an Unshakable Life is a book written for those in the trenches of real life. It is written for those who have or are facing challenges, surprises, disappointments, success and failures. When life comes at you fast and hard, when your world is shaken, where do you stand?

David was a man who understood life-shaking experiences. Life had thrown all types of pressures at him: failure, success, friends, betrayal, attack, discouragement, fear, hope, loss of a vision. He had faced the natural Goliaths and the spiritual Goliaths in his life and learned how to renew his strength, how to find his help in God and how to stand strong.

Psalm 27 is David's faith declarations for seasons of shaking. They are the principles he lived by when life was unexplainable and overwhelming. In Psalm 27 we learn how David built an unshakable life on the unshakable word of God.

You too can build an unshakable life, a life that is anchored, immovable and indestructible. The seven declarations from Psalm 27 are for your journey and my journey. Join with me as we develop each one of these seven declarations for an unshakable life:

I will live life strong.
I will love God's house.
I will hold my head high.
I will have an overflowing heart.
I will turn to God at all times.
I will walk on a level path.
I will not lose heart.

This book will change the way you live!
Frank Damazio

Psalm 27

The Lord is my light and my salvation;
Whom shall I fear?
The Lord is the strength of my life;
Of whom shall I be afraid?

When the wicked came against me
To eat up my flesh,
My enemies and foes,
They stumbled and fell.

Though an army may encamp against me,
My heart shall not fear;
Though war may rise against me,
In this I will be confident.

One thing I have desired of the Lord,
That will I seek:
That I may dwell in the house of the Lord
All the days of my life,
To behold the beauty of the Lord,
And to inquire in His temple.

For in the time of trouble
He shall hide me in His pavilion;
In the secret place of His tabernacle
He shall hide me;
He shall set me high upon a rock.

And now my head shall be lifted up above my enemies all
around me;

Therefore I will offer sacrifices of joy in His tabernacle;
I will sing, yes, I will sing praises to the Lord.

Hear, O Lord, when I cry with my voice!
Have mercy also upon me, and answer me.

When You said, "Seek My face,"
My heart said to You, "Your face, Lord, I will seek."

Do not hide Your face from me;
Do not turn Your servant away in anger;
You have been my help;
Do not leave me nor forsake me,
O God of my salvation.

When my father and my mother forsake me,
Then the Lord will take care of me.

Teach me Your way, O Lord,
And lead me in a smooth path, because of my enemies.

Do not deliver me to the will of my adversaries;
For false witnesses have risen against me,
And such as breathe out violence.

I would have lost heart, unless I had believed
That I would see the goodness of the Lord
In the land of the living.

Wait on the Lord;
Be of good courage,
And He shall strengthen your heart;
Wait, I say, on the Lord.

The Unshakable Life

An unshakable life is built on the unshakable Word of God. It becomes a life that is anchored, immovable and indestructible.

Chapter 1

The Unshakable Life

One sure thing about life is its constant uncertainty. Life changes all around us and some of these changes shatter our world: the bad news from the doctor, the job layoff, the son who drops out of school, the business that ends with bankruptcy, the secret habit that is publicly exposed. Shaken. Crushed. Fallen apart.

The immovable, unshakable life is not a life without problems but a life lived above these problems through a living faith in God and faith in the scriptures. It is a faith that plants your feet on solid ground and refuses to be moved. Undefeatable, unbeaten.

The unshakable person is one who learns how to fill his or her heart and mouth with unshakable declarations built upon the scriptures. My goal is to change the way you respond to any and all life challenges by changing your words and the way you speak. I want to encourage you to fill your heart and your mouth with faith declarations, words that are true because God says they are true, words that shape your life into an unshakable life filled with the blessings and the favor of God.

In the following chapters, we will cover seven unshakable life declarations given to us in Psalm 27:1-14, a Psalm of David. David was a survivor of life crises, a person who learned unshakable life declarations from the hardships, surprises, contradictions, losses, sorrows and challenges of life.

Ground-Shaking Earthquakes

In 1995, disaster struck Kobe, Japan, and injured 33,000, killed 5,470, left 300,000 homeless and destroyed an estimated 144,000 buildings. What caused such massive devastation? The ground shook. It didn't shake very long—only 20 seconds. But in those 20 seconds of ground-shaking, hundreds of thousands of lives were destroyed.

Because of earthquake devastation like this, scientists have been working on techniques for building earthquake resistant buildings. Their goal is to build structures that have the strength, flexibility and proper foundation to withstand the forces of nature. In the same way, an unshakable life must be built on a foundation that can withstand world forces.

The Unshakable Life is Built on the Unshakable Word

Psalm 27 (see pages 6 and 7) is the quake-resistant foundation that shows us how to live and not be shaken by the things happening around us. We can have an unshakable life when enemies of our soul rise up against us, when people attack us, when spiritual darkness threatens to overwhelm us. We can have an unshakable life.

An unshakable life is built on the unshakable Word of God. It becomes a life that is anchored, immovable and indestructible. When unforeseen catastrophes attack, an unshakable life remains steadfast. When storms bear down with hurricane force winds and devastating floods, an unshakable life reaches down into the bedrock and gains strength to stand unbeaten.

Shake-Resistant Lives

Luke 6:48 tells of a man "building a house, who dug deep and laid the foundation on the rock. And when the flood arose, the stream beat vehemently against that house, and could not shake it, for it was founded on the rock."

Just as this man was building a house, you are building your life. No one else can live your life but you. No one else can build its foundation but you. You build by the decisions you make, the character you develop, the attitudes you cultivate. If you want an unshakable life, you have to dig deep and lay your foundation on the rock.

Life-Shaking Tests and Trials

Your life will be shaken by tests, trials and temptations. Tests and trials prove the quality and worth of something. 1 Corinthians 3:12-15 says, "Now if anyone builds on this foundation with gold, silver, precious stones, wood, hay, straw, each one's work will become clear; for the Day will declare it, because it will be revealed by fire; and the fire will test each one's work, of what sort it is. If anyone's work which he has built on it endures, he will receive a reward. If anyone's work is burned, he will suffer loss; but he himself will be saved, yet so as through fire." Tests come to validate the quality of the foundation. The purpose is not to destroy the foundation, but to establish its strength.

Tests reveal what is important.

True values surface after spiritual testing. They refine your character and life. The things that are unimportant, superficial or wrong get stripped away. The part of your life that is left is the genuine part, the part that is like Christ, the part that continues to trust God.

James 1:3-4 tells us, "For when your faith is tested, your endurance has a chance to grow. So let it grow, for when your endurance is fully developed, you will be strong in character and ready for anything" (New Living Translation).

Trials prove the genuineness of our faith.

1 Peter 1:6-8 tells of the testing of genuine faith: "In this you greatly rejoice, though now for a little while, if need be, you have been grieved by various trials, that the genuineness of your faith, being much more precious than gold that perishes, though it is tested by fire, may be found to praise, honor, and glory at the revelation of Jesus Christ, whom having not seen you love."

Your faith is known to be genuine because it has been tested and proved to be the real thing. It can be given a certificate of authenticity as genuine faith. It isn't just lip-service faith that says the right thing but believes another. It is faith that goes to the core of your nature, faith that has dug down to the bedrock of your life and built on the unchangeable nature of God.

Author Lee Strobel put it this way: "A faith that's challenged by adversity or tough questions or contemplation is often a stronger faith in the end."[1]

Trials expose the content of your heart.

In Deuteronomy 8:2, Moses tells Israel that God led them through the wilderness for 40 years "to test you, to know what was in your heart, whether you would keep His commandments or not." Later he says, "The Lord your God is testing you to know whether you love the Lord your God with all your heart and with all your soul" (Deuteronomy 13:3).

This is repeated throughout scripture. God tests men to prove what is in their hearts. He already knows, but He wants them to see it as well. (See also 2 Chronicles 32:31; Psalm 7:9; 11:5.)

Job and his wife went through the same tests. They lost their children, lost their possessions, and lost their wealth. Job was tried one step further and lost his health, but still Job's response was "Shall we indeed accept good from God, and shall we not accept adversity?" (Job 2:10). His wife's response was "Curse God and die" (Job 2:9).

The same trials came but one proved to have corruption in her heart and the other did not. Job's wife became angry and bitter toward God. She turned her back on God. Job's response was, "I trust God." What is your response at the unexpected trials of life? Curse God or trust God? Maybe you don't curse God with swear words, but you can speak negatively about God, question His faithfulness, question His love, question who He is. Or you can believe the truth of His unchanging nature as seen in the Word of God and with Job boldly say, "He is my God. I will trust Him no matter what happens in life." (See Job 13:15.)

Trials purify and sanctify your motivation.

John wanted something from Jesus. In Mark 10:35-37 he and his brother came to Jesus and asked, "Teacher, we want You to do for us whatever we ask." Then they proceeded to ask to sit at the right and left hand of Jesus when He was glorified.

Many years and many trials later, we see a different John. Instead of the John asking to be in a position of power, we see the John of 1 John who rejoices in being a child of God. Nowhere in any of his three epistles do you see the attitude of pride and position that is so blatant in Mark 10. Instead we hear the voice of one who is quietly confident in His God. We hear the heart of love for others and love for God. No striving for position, we only find a passion to serve.

John always loved God and always wanted to serve, but earlier in his life his motivation was impure, tainted with his carnal desires. Later, John demonstrates a purity of heart that exemplified the principle Jesus gave him in Mark 10:43-45: "Whoever desires to become great among you shall be your servant. And whoever of you desires to be first shall be slave of all. For even the Son of Man did not come to be served, but to serve, and to give His life a ransom for many."

Trials call into exercise the graces of the Spirit.

Over and over Paul rejoices in his trials because it was through them he found a place of sufficiency and trust in God. When the trials became great, he found God's grace to be greater still. In 2 Corinthians 3:5, he says, "Not that we are sufficient of ourselves to think of anything as being from ourselves, but our sufficiency is from God." And in 2 Corinthians 12:10, "Therefore I take pleasure in infirmities, in reproaches, in needs, in persecutions, in distresses, for Christ's sake. For when I am weak, then I am strong."

Hebrews 4:16 urges us to "come boldly to the throne of grace, that we may obtain mercy and find grace to help in time of need." It doesn't matter what the infirmities, reproaches, needs, persecutions and distresses are. You come to a throne of grace. You come to a Sovereign Lord who reigns in power and grace. It is there you find all the help we need. It is there you find the sufficiency to stand firm in any life-shaking.

Tests form Christ's character in you.

Tests bring you to maturity. They expose your weaknesses and strengthen you to become more like Him. In Psalm 17:3 David says, "You have tested my heart; you have visited me in the night; you have tried me and have found nothing; I have purposed that my mouth shall not transgress." His conclusion of the chapter is the heart desire of every one of us. "As for me,

I will see Your face in righteousness; I shall be satisfied when I awake in Your likeness" (Psalm 17:15). When shaking comes to your life, it forces you to evaluate our foundation, to look again at the underpinnings of your life and to reinforce the things you hold as important. At the end, you can look back with David and say, "I am becoming more like Christ."

Tests cultivate a deeper understanding of God's ways and character.

At the end of Job's tests, he summarizes everything that had happened in one simple yet profound sentence. "I had heard about you before, but now I have seen you with my own eyes" (Job 42:5, *New Living Translation*). You can believe in the love of God, but when you depend on that love for your strength, it becomes real. You can believe in the sovereignty of God, but not until you have stood in anguish and confusion and declared your trust does it become confirmed in you.

In Romans 8:38-39, Paul passionately declares, "For I am persuaded that neither death nor life, nor angels nor principalities nor powers, nor things present nor things to come, nor height nor depth, nor any other created thing, shall be able to separate us from the love of God which is in Christ Jesus our Lord."

These are powerful words, but in times of life-shaking, they can become more than just words. They become the very breath that sustains you. They are the bedrock under your feet that surges life into you when your world begins to shake. You no longer read them as simply beautiful-sounding verses from the Bible. They become a powerful force in your heart that bursts from your mouth into a faith declaration that you throw into the face of the enemy: "I am absolutely convinced, beyond the shadow of a doubt. I base my very existence on this confident determination that there is absolutely nothing – no disease, not even death itself – that can separate me from God's love. Nothing that happens in life – loss, abuse, betrayal, no crime or sin committed against me – there is absolutely nothing that could ever snatch me out of the loving arms of the Almighty God."

What has changed those from being words to being a declaration are the trials that brought a deeper, life-transforming understanding of the character and ways of God.

God Is in Control

Never forget that tests and trials originate with God. Whatever circumstances you come through, whatever form the shakings may take, remember that God is always in control. When Satan wanted to test Job, he had to go through God first. No matter the situation you find yourself in, God is still in control of it.

Floods will come to your life. Storms will beat against it. You can get hammered by a situation mentally, emotionally, spiritually, domestically, relationally, financially, until you feel you cannot stand. You can be under attack and discouraged. Maybe you have lost vision and confidence. You have lost your way and the spirit of faith has been beat out of you.

You need to build into your life an absolute confidence, an absolute faith in God, that you will not be shaken in any situation. No matter the size of the earthquake in your life, you can be built on a bedrock foundation that will not move. Psalm 16:8 says, "I have set the Lord always before me; because He is at my right hand I shall not be moved." You shall not be moved. Your house will not be shaken and destroyed. You can trust your God. Plant your feet on the rock and let the storms come because you will not be moved.

Camey was two years old when she was first diagnosed with cancer. Over the next 21 years she spent a good portion of her life in the hospital, undergoing surgeries and chemo-therapy. At the age of 23 she wrote, "I know there are many who have pitied my beginnings, thinking it tragic that I had to endure such traumas both as a child and throughout my life, but I confess that I have rather pitied those who have never tasted the bitterness of a trial 'too severe.' For how is one to appreciate the contrast of light's dawning hope if his soul has never trembled through the dark hours of a nightmare watch? Or how can one prove God's faithfulness if he never is granted the privilege of wandering through a barren desert where only pools of God's presence can possibly provide survival?"[2]

Psalm 55:22 counsels us to "Cast your burden on the Lord, and He shall sustain you; He shall never permit the righteous to be moved." He will never, never, never, never permit the righteous to be moved. Never, not ever. Through God you will stand firm and strong, unshaken and immovable through the storms that come.

The Unshakable Life

An unshakable life is built on the unshakable Word of God. It becomes a life that is anchored, immovable and indestructible.

An Unshakable Life Declaration

An unshakable life is built on the unshakable Word of God. It becomes a life that is anchored, immovable and indestructible as we speak faith declarations from the Word.

Chapter 2

An Unshakable Life Speaks Faith Declarations

ords are powerful. One conversation with a person can turn a good day into a terrible day. One sentence from a friend at the right time can turn a hopeless situation into one filled with hope. The right words from a coach can turn a team from defeated losers into aggressive players. Psychologists at the University of Denver studied newlyweds over the first ten years of their marriage to see if there was a way to tell at the beginning of the marriage if the relationship would last or not. They found one key factor: the number of insults or putdowns the couples would say to each other. Among couples who would stay together, the number was 5 percent; among couples who would divorce, it was 10 percent. That percentage grew each year until at the end of 10 years the couples who would divorce were insulting each other five times more often than couples who would remain married.[1] They were only words, yet they destroyed marriages.

Words have power over your life and your future. When God created the world, He spoke the creative word and the result was the creation that we see. Words have creative power – power to do good or to do harm, power to give life or power to destroy.

I want to challenge you to change your words. Change the way you speak about your life. Change what you say about God. Fill your mouth with the Word of God and begin to speak it daily. Don't allow life to shape your words but shape your life with your words.

A Faith Declaration

A faith declaration is a declaration of the absolute faithfulness of God's word. Believing God's word isn't enough. You must declare it. Speak it. God wants you to change the way you talk and the words that are in your mouth.

Hebrews 4:14 says, "Let us hold fast our confession." In the Greek, the verb "hold fast" means to cause something to continue happening on the basis of some authority or power. We are to hold fast to our confession. This isn't a one-time thing but it is an ongoing habit, a way of living. We make a decision to confess the word of God, to say the same thing that God's word says, and we continue doing that because of the power and authority of that Word. Make that decision today: "I will hold fast to my confession of the Word of God. I will not waver. I will not give up. I will continually speak the truth of God's Word."

A faith declaration is made when you declare the absolute faithfulness of God's Word.

A faith declaration is not positive speaking. It is not simply speaking positive words about whatever you want to happen. It is speaking the Word of God. A faith declaration is based in the Word of God. When Jesus was attacked by the devil, He said, "It is written." He used the word of God and He spoke it. He didn't just think it. He put the words from His heart into His mouth and spoke them.

You can't speak His Word if it isn't in you. You can't declare the Word of God if you don't know what it is. Colossians 3:16 says, "Let the word of Christ dwell in you richly in all wisdom, teaching and admonishing one another in psalms and hymns and spiritual songs, singing with grace in your hearts to the Lord." You need to have the Word of God in your heart. It needs to live there. The Word of God can't be a weekend visitor to your life. It can't be something you invite in for holidays and special occasions. It needs to have a permanent address in your heart.

God's Word is faithful. It doesn't change. We can trust it. Psalm 119:138 states, "Your testimonies, which You have commanded, are righteous and very faithful." We can depend on it. God's word isn't going to change tomorrow. It is here to stay and it is unchanging. Everything around us changes. People change. What they say about us changes. Our life situations change. Things begin to shake. The earth begins to move and everything around us begins to wobble and then to shake, but one thing stands firm – the Word of God. It isn't affected by life struggles. It isn't affected by life changes. It is unmoving, stable, dependable, and trustworthy.

Psalm 46:1-3 is our unshakable truth. "God is our refuge and strength, a very present help in trouble. Therefore we will not fear, even though the earth be removed, and though the mountains be carried into the midst of the sea; though its waters roar and be troubled, though the mountains shake with its swelling."

A faith declaration is made when your heart and mouth agree together with the truth.

In Matthew 12:34, Jesus says, "Out of the abundance of the heart the mouth speaks." Your heart and your mouth are connected. That which is in your heart will come out your mouth, so what is in your heart? Make sure your heart is not filled with things that you don't want to come out of your mouth. Fill your heart with the Word of God. Deuteronomy 30:14 and Romans 10:8 tell us, "The word is very near you, in your mouth and in your heart that you may do it."

Romans 10:9-10 continues, "if you confess with your mouth the Lord Jesus and believe in your heart that God has raised Him from the dead, you will be saved. For with the heart one believes unto righteousness, and with the mouth confession is made unto salvation."

Salvation is your first faith declaration. You declare with your mouth what your heart believes. You believe in your heart that Jesus is Lord and declare it with your mouth." Don't stop there though. Keep believing what the Word of God says and keep declaring it.

Study the Word of God and memorize it. Memorization is a difficult thing in our culture. We aren't used to memorizing anything. Why memorize statistics when you can Google them in a minute? Why memorize telephone numbers when your cell phone does it for you?

When you memorize something, you write it in your mind in indelible ink. I challenge you to begin an active, purposeful scripture memorization program today. The Word of God needs to be written into your heart in indelible ink so you can speak it out of your mouth without even thinking. It's good to read what other people have written. It's good to read books and listen to sermons. But these cannot and never will take the place of reading and studying and memorizing the Word of God for yourself. God doesn't want to speak to you secondhand. He wants to speak from His Word directly to your heart. Then those words can come from your heart through your lips and shape your life and your environment.

A faith declaration is made when you speak God's Word with a spirit of faith.

The two key words in Romans 10:9-10 are *believe* in your heart and *confess* with your mouth. Believe and confess. You cannot simply say the words without believing them.

2 Corinthians 4:13 repeats this thought: "And since we have the same spirit of faith, according to what is written, 'I believed and therefore I spoke,' we also believe and therefore speak."

Believe and speak. Memorize the Word of God and put it in your heart. That's what Moses commanded Joshua in Joshua 1:8, "This Book of the Law shall not depart from your mouth, but you shall meditate in it day and night." But Moses doesn't end there. He goes on to say, "That you may observe to do according to all that is written in it. For then you will make your way prosperous and then you will have good success."

You can't just meditate on the Word of God; you must believe it and act on it. Do you believe? Then speak what you believe. Then act on it. Obey it. If you do, the Bible promises you will have a successful life journey.

A faith declaration affirms what you believe and stand upon.

You have just been told that you have cancer, that you have been fired, that your business is going under. What do you do? What are the words that come out of your mouth? Job's wife quickly spoke what was in her heart, "Curse God and die." That is one option, but it isn't the one I want to choose. I prefer what was in Job's heart. "He fell to the ground and worshiped. And he said: 'Naked I came from my mother's womb, and naked shall I return there. The Lord gave, and the Lord has taken away; Blessed be the name of the Lord.'" (Job 1:20-21)

What did Job believe? He believed that God was to be worshipped, to be blessed, and to be trusted. And those were the words that came from his mouth.

What comes from your mouth when everything around you begins to fall apart? What words do you speak when your husband leaves or your child dies? Why not say, "I will say of the Lord, 'He is my refuge and my fortress. My God, in Him I will trust'" (Psalm 91:2).

We don't have to understand why things are happening. In fact, we often don't. There can be no explanations that make sense in the crisis moment, but we have one truth, one unshakable and unchangeable truth, that we can hold to: He is trustworthy. There is a better chance of the Rocky Mountains moving to Hawaii than there is of God stopping loving us. " 'Even if the mountains walk away and the hills fall to pieces, My love won't walk away from you, my covenant commitment of peace won't fall apart.' The God who has compassion on you says so" (Isaiah 54:10, *The Message*). He said it. Now you declare it.

A faith declaration expands the boundaries of your life.

A faith declaration fixes the landmarks of my life. In the Old Testament landmarks were boundary lines. They marked where a family's inheritance stopped and started. With your words you can enlarge your future or shrink it. Your words can enlarge the possibilities of your life or destroy your spirit of faith. God can open the door, but if you live in fear, you won't walk through it. You can have a pessimistic attitude about your life that does not believe the Word of God and you won't be able to see what God is doing in your life. He can open a door and you'll never see it. You can limit what God wants to do in your life through your confession because you will not believe what He wants to do.

Have the attitude of Jabez. His words were words of faith and trust in God that enlarged the boundary lines of his life. He prayed, "Oh, that You would bless me indeed, and enlarge my territory, that Your hand would be with me, and that You would keep me from evil, that I may not cause pain!" (1 Chronicles 4:10). God's response was to give him what he asked for.

A faith declaration sows word-seed that will bring a harvest.

Your words can be seeds. Sow these seeds of faith into your future and see what harvest God will bring. If you sow words of unbelief, your future will be one of unbelief. If you sow words of faith, your destiny will be a faith-filled destiny of great harvest. If you sow words of bitterness and anger, you will reap broken relationships. If you sow mercy, you will receive mercy.

The principle of sowing and reaping is a biblical principle. Isaiah 30:23 says, "Then He will give the rain for your seed with which you sow the ground, and bread of the increase of the earth; it will be fat and plentiful." If a farmer wants a harvest of wheat, he doesn't sow cotton. If you want a harvest of healthy relationships, you can't sow jealousy. If you want to be a person of faith in the future, you have to speak words of faith now.

A faith declaration builds your spirit and faith to a higher level.

Read this verse and think about it. "But you, beloved, building yourselves up on your most holy faith, praying in the Holy Spirit" (Jude 20). To build yourself up you have to fill your life with the Word of God. You have to start speaking the Word, confessing the Word, believing the Word.

Romans 10:17 says that faith comes by hearing and speaking the Word of God. You can't hear what has not been spoken, so speak the Word and listen to yourself speaking it. Begin to make faith declarations about your life. Stop believing the negative. Stop believing things that are not biblical. Build your life on the Word of God and change your speech to be in agreement with what God says.

Maybe you are already doing this, then do it more. Go to the next level. Speak the Word more, memorize the Word more, and believe the Word more. Don't be satisfied where you are. God has more for you, so take a step up, then another one, then another one. Don't stop! He wants you to grow into much more than you would believe.

A faith declaration shows trust of God's involvement in your life and belief that He wants the best for you.

I know you have read Jeremiah 29:11, but read it again out loud as if you have never heard these words before. "I know the thoughts that I think toward you, says the Lord, thoughts of peace and not of evil, to give you a future and a hope." Everything that He thinks about you, every plan He has for you, is the absolute best that He can think of for your life. He never thinks of the least He can do for you, but of the most. Every path He has prepared for you is the absolute best that He can think of for you.

He is a good God who loves you more than you can begin to understand. He is an awesome God and you can trust Him. You can trust His will. His will for your life is not just good, it is the best. He will enlarge your borders, broaden your destiny, and plan great things for your future.

Don't Give Up Your Faith Declaration

Job's life-shaking events all happened in one day. When he woke up in the morning he was one of the richest men in the world. He had "seven thousand sheep, three thousand camels, five hundred yoke of oxen, five hundred female donkeys, and a very large household, so that this man was the greatest of all the people of the East" (Job 1:2).

Job was the biblical Bill Gates. He was wealthy – very wealthy. Not only that, but he was well respected. Everyone talked about his philanthropy toward the widows and the poor. He was known for his wisdom and people came to seek his counsel. And he had a great family—seven sons and three daughters. They were doing quite well too—good kids, got along well, owned their own homes. They were a close-knit family, getting together for family dinners frequently.

When Job went to bed that night, his wealth disintegrated, his home was destroyed and his children died. As for his stellar reputation, his three good friends came over to console him in his grief by telling him what a rotten person he was.

What do you do when you have made a faith declaration and suddenly the earth begins to shake? Things have been very quiet and peaceful, but you took a stand and the earthquake started. Don't be defeated by doubt and negativity. Don't allow yourself to begin to question the Word of God and doubt what He has said. Proverbs 6:2 says we can be snared by the words we speak. We can be captured by them. Don't let that happen.

Fear can begin to whisper into your ear. If you listen, you will begin to speak what you are hearing instead of what God is saying. Maybe you are struggling in your marriage and hear the word "divorce" whispering into your dreams. Maybe you are struggling with purity and are beginning to rationalize what the Word of God says. Put the following scriptures into your heart and declare them out loud. Take a stand.

Psalm 17:3
"You have tested my heart; You have visited me in the night; You have tried me and have found nothing; I have purposed that my mouth shall not transgress."

Psalm 19:14
"Let the words of my mouth and the meditation of my heart be acceptable in Your sight, O Lord, my strength and my Redeemer."

Psalm 141:3

"Set a guard, O Lord, over my mouth; keep watch over the door of my lips."

Proverbs 12:14

"A man will be satisfied with good by the fruit of his mouth, and the recompense of a man's hands will be rendered to him."

Proverbs 13:3

"He who guards his mouth preserves his life, but he who opens wide his lips shall have destruction."

Proverbs 21:23

"Whoever guards his mouth and tongue keeps his soul from troubles."

Isaiah 6:7

"And he touched my mouth with it, and said: 'Behold, this has touched your lips; your iniquity is taken away, and your sin purged.'"

David's Life-Shaking Years

David's shaking lasted longer than one day. It was an ongoing stress on his life. He had faithfully served King Saul, risking his life to fight Saul's battles for him. He showed great loyalty to Saul, never undermining his authority. You would think Saul would show him a little bit of appreciation. Instead, Saul tried to kill him and David's life-shaking years began. He ran to the wilderness to hide from this madman who was trying to destroy his life. For years he lived without his childhood friends, without his family, without any possessions to call his own.

It's hard to make a good living when you are living in caves, running from one place to another with an angry king and your heels. So David lived years of shaking, separated from his home and family and childhood friends, in fear for his life, without hope for his future.

David's Life Declarations

What kind of life declarations comes from David's mouth as a result of these life-shaking events? "Woe is me. Life is miserable. God has forgotten me. I'm a victim of a mad king and unfair life circumstances. I didn't do anything to deserve this. It's not fair."

That's not what I read in Psalm 27. Look at the statements David makes: "My strength is in God. My hope is in God. I will praise God. I will seek Him. I will trust Him." He takes an unwavering and unshakable stand in the face of adverse circumstances and declares out loud the principles that hold his life steady.

Ask God right now to purge your lips, to touch your speech with His holy Word and keep your mouth from speaking things that are not in agreement with the Word of God. Set a guard over your mouth and do not let anything slip out that is not of God. Draw a line in the sand today. Behind you are the negative words of the past. Behind you are the doubts and fears of yesterday. From this day on begin to speak faith, begin to speak the unshakable Word of God over your life.

Seven Unshakable Life Declarations

The seven unshakable life declarations from Psalm 27 are:

▶ *1. I will live life strong.*

Psalm 27:1-3
"The Lord is my light and my salvation; whom shall I fear? The Lord is the strength of my life; of whom shall I be afraid? When the wicked came against me to eat up my flesh, my enemies and foes, they stumbled and fell. Though an army may encamp against me, my heart shall not fear; Though war may rise against me, in this I will be confident."

▶ *2. I will love God's house passionately.*

Psalm 27:4-5
"One thing I have desired of the Lord, that will I seek: that I may dwell in the house of the Lord all the days of my life, to behold the beauty of the Lord, and to inquire in His temple. For in the time of trouble He shall hide me in His pavilion; in the secret place of His tabernacle He shall hide me; He shall set me high upon a rock."

▶ *3. I will hold my head high.*

Psalm 27:6
"And now my head shall be lifted up above my enemies all around me; Therefore I will offer sacrifices of joy in His tabernacle; I will sing, yes, I will sing praises to the Lord."

▶ *4. I will have an overflowing heart.*

Psalm 27:7-8

"Hear, O Lord, when I cry with my voice! Have mercy also upon me, and answer me. When You said, 'Seek My face,' my heart said to You, 'Your face, Lord, I will seek.'"

▶ *5. I will turn to God at all times.*

Psalm 27:9-10

"Do not hide Your face from me; Do not turn Your servant away in anger; You have been my help; Do not leave me nor forsake me, O God of my salvation. When my father and my mother forsake me, then the Lord will take care of me."

▶ *6. I will walk on a level path.*

Psalm 27:11-12

"Teach me Your way, O Lord, and lead me in a smooth path, because of my enemies. Do not deliver me to the will of my adversaries; for false witnesses have risen against me, and such as breathe out violence."

▶ *7. I will not lose heart.*

Psalm 27:13-14

"I would have lost heart, unless I had believed that I would see the goodness of the Lord In the land of the living. Wait on the Lord; Be of good courage, and He shall strengthen your heart; Wait, I say, on the Lord!"

I Will Live Life Strong

I will not faint or be feeble. I will have strength and power greater than average or what is expected. I will be able to stand firm and to sustain any and all attacks. I will endure because I am established and well-fortified in my God.

Psalm 27:1-3
"The Lord is my light and my salvation; whom shall I fear? The Lord is the strength of my life; of whom shall I be afraid? When the wicked came against me to eat up my flesh, my enemies and foes, they stumbled and fell. Though an army may encamp against me, my heart shall not fear; Though war may rise against me, in this I will be confident."

Chapter 3

I Will Live Life Strong

The unshakable life is built upon the unshakable Word of God and unshakable life declarations. Because we all feel shakable and weak at times, it is important to live by the Word of God. Matthew 26:41 says, "Watch and pray lest you enter into temptation. The spirit indeed is willing but the flesh is weak."

Our spirit is willing to be strengthened and is willing to do what is right. The problem is our lower nature, our old self, that part of us that is rooted in sin and shaped in iniquity. Our flesh is weak, does not desire spiritual things and will not push us to live life strong.

We must, with the apostle Paul, make this confession: "Therefore I take pleasure in infirmities and reproaches, in needs, in persecutions, in distresses, for Christ's sake. For when I am weak, then I am strong" (2 Corinthians 12:10). Out of our weakness, we choose to draw on the strength of our God.

David wrote these words for all who choose to live life strong. "The Lord is my light and my salvation; whom shall I fear? The Lord is the strength of my life; of whom shall I be afraid? When the wicked came against me to eat up my flesh, my enemies and foes, they stumbled and fell. Though an army may encamp against me, my heart shall not fear; Though war may rise against me, in this I will be confident" (Psalm 27:1-3).

David was under attack by armies that outnumbered him. He had more enemies than he could imagine, yet he made a choice. He made a decision to live life strong. Like David, we have a choice. We can live in weakness, fear, unbelief and drained of all our strength or we can choose to live strong in this power of God's might and in His strength.

Psalm 27 is written by David as a song of confidence that demonstrates how a person facing troubles responds with an absolute faith declaration, a confession that establishes his direction and attitude. This is a psalm that records the triumph of a warrior's faith. Let it inspire you to live a life with unshakable life declarations in your heart and mouth.

When you face life's challenges, surprises and overwhelming storms that seek to shake the ground you stand on, you must have unshakable life declarations. Your words are powerful. Your words can snare you and hold you in captivity or they can set you free and enlarge your spiritual capacity. Your confession sets a mark on your life that builds you up or tears you down.

What Does It Mean to Live Strong?

Living life strong is to live with this declaration in your heart and mouth: "I will not faint or be feeble. I will have strength and power greater than average or what is expected. I will be able to stand firm and to sustain any and all attacks. I will endure because I am established and well-fortified in my God."

You have a choice. You can choose to live life strong or you can choose to live life defeated. Instead of making a living strong declaration, you can make a declaration of a weak life: "I will life live defeated, discouraged and depressed. I will live a life of disappointment and regret. Life is so hard I can't overcome. When attacks come, I will just try to survive, to 'get by' and hope that maybe one day things might get better."

It's Your Choice

You choose. How do you want to live life? Maybe life has shaken your confidence. Maybe people and circumstances have limited your vision for your life. You have given up hope and are hanging on by your fingertips. Make a choice now.

Isaiah 35:3-4 urges us to "Strengthen the weak hands, and make firm the feeble knees. Say to those who are fearful-hearted, 'Be strong, do not fear! Behold, your God will come with vengeance, with the recompense of God; He will come and save you.'"

In Deuteronomy 31:6, we are also encouraged to "Be strong and of good courage, do not fear nor be afraid of them; for the Lord your God, He is the One who goes with you. He will not leave you nor forsake you."

God repeats this over and over throughout scripture. "Be strong and I will be with you. Be strong and I will work on your behalf." Make a decision to stand strong and to live life strong. When you do, you will find that you are not standing alone. God is there with you. It is His strength. It is His power and His might that will empower you (Ephesians 6:10; 2 Timothy 2:1). Stand strong and He will work on your behalf.

Joseph chose to live strong when under attack.

Genesis 49:23-24 promises strength to those who turn to God: "The archers have bitterly grieved him, shot at him and hated him. But his bow remained in strength, and the arms of his hands were made strong by the hands of the Mighty God of Jacob."

Joseph was attacked and betrayed by those closest to him—his own family. He was lied about, slandered, mis-treated, and wrongfully imprisoned. He had every reason to be angry and bitter. Instead he chose to live in a place of strength.

"Remained" in the Hebrew can be translated "to live or dwell in a house." He was strengthened in His God and lived strong.

Joshua chose to live strong when under pressure.

In Joshua 1:6-9, God inspires Joshua to stand strong against what appears to be undefeatable obstacles: "Be strong and of good courage, for to this people you shall divide as an inheritance the land which I swore to their fathers to give them. Only be strong and very courageous, that you may observe to do according to all the law which Moses My servant commanded you; do not turn from it to the right hand or to the left, that you may prosper wherever you go…. Have I not commanded you? Be strong and of good courage; do not be afraid, nor be dismayed, for the Lord your God is with you wherever you go."

Joshua had just been placed in charge of an entire nation. The nation of Israel was looking to him for direction and leadership. In front of him was a land occupied by giants who had no intention of peacefully allowing the Israelites to move into the neighborhood. He was under pressure, but he stood strong in the confidence that God was with Him. Instead of living in fear of the size of his enemy, he lived in confidence in the presence of his God.

Caleb lived strong when the vision was delayed.

Caleb was 85 years old when he declared in Joshua 14:11: "As yet I am as strong this day as on the day that Moses sent me; just as my strength was then, so now is my strength for war, both for going out and for coming in."

For 40 years Caleb thought about the land that he had seen. For 40 years he remembered the promise of God. When the Israelites began their conquest of Canaan, Caleb went after that promise. He pursued that vision. He did not allow time to drain his strength. He did not allow postponement of the vision to discourage him and weaken him. He maintained his strength for 40 years and took possession of the inheritance God had promised.

Joab lived strong when surrounded by the enemy.

Joab was surrounded on all sides when he told his troops in 2 Samuel 10:12: "Be of good courage, and let us be strong for our people and for the cities of our God. And may the Lord do what is good in His sight."

Joab had the Ammonites in front of him and the Syrians behind him, but he didn't give up. He joined his strength with the strength of his brother and went to battle. He didn't fight alone. In verse eleven he said to his brother, "If the Syrians are too strong for me, then you shall help me; but if the people of Ammon are too strong for you, then I will come and help you." When surrounded by the enemy, Joab found strength in unity and relationship.

Asa chose to live strong when completing what he started.

The Lord encouraged Asa in 2 Chronicles 15:7, 8: " 'But you, be strong and do not let your hands be weak, for your work shall be rewarded!' And when Asa heard these words … he took courage…"

When Asa became king, he began to rebuild the country, fortifying the cities and removing the altars to false gods. In the middle of his rebuilding he was attacked by enemies that outnumbered him two to one, but Asa did not "let his hands be weak." The idea here is of abandoning what he had begun. When the enemy attacked, when the building took longer than he thought, he didn't give up. He didn't abandon the purposes of God. He remained strong and God rewarded his work.

Hezekiah lived strong when his trust in God was tested.

Marching into battle, King Hezekiah urged his troops in 2 Chronicles 32:7-8 to "'Be strong and courageous; do not be afraid nor dismayed before the king of Assyria, nor before all the multitude that is with him; for there are more with us than with him. With him is an arm of flesh; but with us is the Lord our God, to help us and to fight our battles.' And the people were strengthened by the words of Hezekiah king of Judah."

When Sennacherib, the king of Assyria, marched against Hezekiah, he began to question Hezekiah's faith and trust in God. "What makes you think God will answer you? Do you really believe He will save you? He hasn't rescued anyone else when I attacked them; what makes you different? Why should He rescue you?" But Hezekiah strengthened his faith in God and trusted in Him. "There are more with us than with him." The enemy may seem great, but God is greater. "Greater is He that is in you than He that is in the world."

Paul lived strong when limitations were placed on him.

In 2 Corinthians 12:10, Paul writes, "Therefore I take pleasure in infirmities, in reproaches, in needs, in persecutions, in distresses, for Christ's sake. For when I am weak, then I am strong."

We look back at the apostle Paul as a great man who wrote a good portion of the New Testament, but the Corinthians looked at him in a different light. In 2 Corinthians 10:10 he quotes them as saying, "'Don't bother about his letters,' some say. 'He sounds big, but it's all noise. When he gets here you will see that there is nothing great about him, and you have never heard a worse preacher!'" (*The Living Bible*)

People were trying to limit Paul, to say he didn't have what it took to accomplish the vision God had given him. They didn't believe in the call of God on His life, but that didn't discourage Paul. It didn't weaken his steadfastness and determination. Instead Paul rejoiced that the strength and power of his ministry was in Christ and not in his own abilities. He placed his focus on Christ and off himself, finding his strength in Christ and not in his own abilities and giftings.

Live Life Strong by Declaring Who God Is

Psalm 27:1
> "The Lord is my light and my salvation. Whom shall I fear? The Lord is the strength of my life, of whom shall I be afraid?"

The Lord is my light.

He is the light that exposes the things in me that need to change. 1 Corinthians 4:5 says God "will both bring to light the hidden things of darkness and reveal the counsels of the hearts." The things that you hide deep inside and hope no one ever finds out, He will bring them to the surface and help you to change. (See also John 8:12; 1 John 1:5.)

The Lord is the light that directs your path. He guides you, removing confusion and bewilderment. He makes your path clear before you. Psalm 119:105 says, "Your word is a lamp to my feet and a light to my path." (See also Psalm 43:3; Proverbs 3:5-6.)

The Lord is my salvation.

In the Hebrew, salvation means deliverance, rescue, salvation, safety, welfare. The Lord is your savior, your redeemer, the one who restores your life. He is your friend and deliverer, your hope and your future. He can solve any problem. He has helped you and He will continue to help you. Psalm 62:2 says, "He only is my rock and my salvation; He is my defense; I shall not be greatly moved." Psalm 118:21 offers similar words: "I will praise You, for You have answered me, and have become my salvation." (See also Exodus 15:2; Psalm 18:2; Psalm 18:46.)

The Lord is my strength.

The Lord is a constant refuge, a place of safety, a stronghold or fortress. 2 Samuel 22:33 declares, "This God is my strong refuge." In His presence, there is a sense of safety and protection.

Why do children run to their parents' room and climb into bed with them when there is a thunderstorm? Do their parents stop the storm? Do they silence the thunder? Children run to their parents' arms because there is a feeling of safety there. Even if the thunder continues to rattle the windows, the child feels safe in daddy's arms. God is your strong refuge. He is the one you can run to when the storm is raging and find comfort and peace in the midst of it.

The Lord is a place of defense, a stronghold. In the Old Testament a stronghold was a fortified city that was designed to protect from enemy attack. It was usually on a high place so they could look out and see the attack coming and prepare before the enemy arrived. God places us on the high place in Him so that we can see and prepare and be ready for the attacks of the enemy. In Psalm 9:9 David declares, "The Lord also will be a refuge for the oppressed, a refuge in times of trouble." And in Psalm 31:2 he prays, "Be my rock of refuge, a fortress of defense to save me."

The Lord is my confidence.

The basis for confidence is trust. In fact our English word "confidence" comes from the Latin word meaning "intense trust." Your confident expectation of living life strong comes from your complete and total trust in God. Psalm 78:7 says,

"That they may set their hope (confidence) in God and not forget the works of God, but keep his commandments."

Where does this hope and confidence come from? Look at Psalm 78:4, "...telling to the generation to come the praises of the Lord, and His strength and His wonderful works that He has done." Fill your heart with the truth of who God is. Read it in the Bible. Look at what He has done. Look at His promises of what He will do. Begin to speak them, to praise God for them. Know His word, believe His word and speak His word. Our confidence and trust in Him is not based on a flimsy spider web of wishes (Job 8:13-14), but on His absolutely unchanging character.

Why do children run to their parents' room when there is a thunderstorm? Do their parents stop the storm? Do they silence the thunder? No. Children run to their parents' arms because there is a feeling of safety there.

You can trust Him. Paul makes an amazing declaration in Romans 8:38. "For I am persuaded..." Persuaded. It is one simple word in English, but in the Greek it paints a powerful picture. Paul is saying, "Everything I know about God has led me to a place of absolute and unwavering conviction. Don't try to convince me otherwise; you can't. Nothing can change what I have come to believe. Nothing in death, nothing in life can shake my conviction. Fear of the future cannot shake my confidence. I have an unwavering, unswerving, unbendable, unfaltering, unshakable confidence in God."

Romans 8:38-39 says, "For I am persuaded that neither death nor life, nor angels nor principalities nor powers, nor things present nor things to come, nor height nor depth, nor any other created thing, shall be able to separate us from the love of God which is in Christ Jesus our Lord."

If you had the same confidence as Paul, how would you live your life differently? If you really believed that God's love for you was unchangeable, that His hand working in your behalf was unshakable, how would you live?

Live Life Strong When Under Attack

Psalm 27:2
"When the wicked came against me to eat up my flesh, my enemies and foes, they stumbled and fell."

We have enemies.

Do you believe that we have enemies? I'm sure your answer is a resounding "yes." We have spiritual enemies. Ephesians 6:12 says, "We do not wrestle against flesh and blood, but against principalities, against powers, against the rulers of the darkness of this age, against spiritual hosts of wickedness in the heavenly places." In 2 Corinthians 10:3 Paul tells us, "Though we walk in the flesh, we do not war according to the flesh."

The devil sets evil strategies in place against us. His strategy in Matthew 13:19 is to quickly snatch away the spiritual seeds that are sown in our hearts through preaching, prayer or God speaking to us. Luke 4:13 says that his strategy is to come again at "an opportune time." He repeatedly comes at our weakest times. He will repeatedly condemn us to shake our assurance, cripple our confidence and devastate our hopes and dreams. He will quietly and persistently take away our spiritual rights and spiritual ground, pushing us back from what God wants for our lives.

2 Corinthians 2:11 says, "We are not unaware of his schemes." He can scheme to overwhelm our soul by a chain of unusual bad experiences, irritations or small calamities and to destroy our faith and overcome us with fear. He can hinder a church from spiritual blessings by creating a spirit of negativism, relational conflicts, spiritual unrest, murmuring, attacking the leaders or anything that will cause division and stop spiritual momentum. Be wise, be aware, be strong.

We have cultural enemies. James 4:4 tells us that the world is at war with God. Our culture does not live according to the standards and truths of God's word, but it attacks those truths constantly. Turn on the television and flip from channel to channel. How many people do you find living according to biblical principles? Browse through the books at the library. How many support the truth of God's word? Listen to the conversations that go on around you on a daily basis. Lay them against the Bible and see if they are saying the same thing. Our culture does not hold to a biblical worldview. Romans 12:2 warns us, "Do not be conformed to this world, but be transformed by the renewing of your mind..."

We have human enemies. There are people who will tell lies about you, try to trip you up, try to alienate you from other people. Perhaps it is someone on your job who is jealous of you because you have the favor of God on your life. Maybe it is someone who is angry because you stand for something that they oppose so they twist your words, slander you, go behind your back to undermine you. Remember, God is for you and God is warring in your behalf (Psalm 55:3, 12-14).

We will be attacked.

We must be aware, be alert for the attacks of the enemy. He will try to crack our foundation of faith. He will try to bring discouragement to weaken our determination to follow the path God has set for us.

He will attack by fear. Fear is a formidable weapon the devil uses against us: fear for our finances, fear for our health, fear for our children, fear for the future, fear of other people. Fear can creep in little by little until it controls our mind, heart and emotions. Fear makes us live with wrong expectations. We expect failure, not success. We expect tragedy, not good. We go through life looking for the bad things so much that we can't see the good things when they are right in front of us.

He will attack by slander. Slander is twisting the truth. People can tell lies against us, speak wrong about us. We can begin to believe the lies and live as if they are true, and we can allow the lies to depress and discourage us so that we give up and quit trying. (See Psalm 71:10; 10:8; 2 Timothy 3:3.)

He will attack with feelings of being overwhelmed. Overwhelmed feelings attack us and work us into a spirit of pessimism. We stop thinking faith thoughts and begin thinking negative thoughts with a negative perspective for a negative outcome. Psalm 143:3-4 says, "For the enemy has persecuted my soul; he has crushed my life to the ground; he has made me dwell in darkness, like those who have long been dead. Therefore my spirit is overwhelmed within me; my heart within me is distressed." (See also Psalm 55:5.)

He will attack by pessimism. We stop believing that God has our best interests in mind and begin drawing restrictions around His possibilities for our life. We begin to expect the worst of life and the worst of God. Pessimism is unbelief and doubt and can harden our heart to a lack of trust in God.

We will not be defeated!

Yes, we have enemies. Yes, we will be attacked. But most absolutely and definitely *yes*, we will not be defeated! David starts out talking about the enemies and foes who attack him, the mighty army that surrounds him, but he doesn't stop there. Our version of Psalm 27 often reads, "When evil people come to destroy me, when my enemies and foes attack me, *I* will stumble and fall. Though a mighty army surrounds me, my heart *lives in fear.* Even if they attack me, I *give up.* "

That's not what David says! "When evil people come to destroy me, when my enemies and foes attack me, *they* will stumble and fall. Though a mighty army surrounds me, *my heart will know no fear.* Even if they attack me, *I remain confident.* "

They will be defeated and unable to carry out their evil plan. Even if it seems like they will succeed, they won't. We will not be destroyed. They will be defeated. They will stumble. They will fall.

Declarations of Living Life Strong

The following six declarations come straight from the Word of God. Each day this week, start your day by stating one of these declarations and memorizing the verse associated with it. Remember, a life declaration is not simply a sentence you repeat. It is a life principle that you live.

I will live strong in the power of God's might and strength.

Ephesians 6:10
> "Finally, my brethren, be strong in the Lord and in the power of His might."

Isaiah 40:25-26 reveals the greatness of the Lord's strength: "'To whom then will you liken Me, or to whom shall I be equal?' says the Holy One. Lift up your eyes on high, and see who has created these things, who brings out their host by number; He calls them all by name, by the greatness of His might and the strength of His power; Not one is missing."

The Lord is all-powerful. No one even comes close to Him in comparison. Isaiah doesn't stop with this declaration of God's greatness. He continues in verses 29-31 by showing how God's greatness touches our lives. "He gives power to the weak, and to those who have no might He increases strength. Even the youths shall faint and be weary, and the young men shall utterly fall, but those who wait on the Lord shall renew their strength; They shall mount up with wings like eagles, they shall run and not be weary, they shall walk and not faint."

Isaiah describes people in three seasons of life. First there are the soarers. Those are the people who are "mounting up with eagles' wings." They are on top of everything. Everything in life is working out for them at that moment. The blessing and favor of God is upon them and they don't have to do anything. They just lock their wings in place and ride the wind to greater heights.

Then there are the runners. Everyone wants to stay in the soaring season, but running seasons come. Sometimes a person isn't soaring on the updrafts, but is running hard and strong. They have hit their stride and are moving strong toward the finish line. Their heads are up and they've got their second wind and are moving confidently forward. People who are weary are using every last ounce of strength. In the running season, God pours in the strength and the runner keeps running without overwhelming exhaustion and hard work.

There is a third season. That's the season of the walkers. When the soarers look down from their lofty place in the heavens, they can see the walkers as failures. The soarer is having blessing after blessing, everything is going right. Remember, we all have seasons of walking. This is hard work. It takes all our strength to keep moving, but we are doing it. This is the uphill part of the marathon as we are aiming for the summit of the mountain. The walker may not be moving quickly, but he's moving. The walking season is a season that takes hard work, but God gives strength so the walker is not fatigued and exhausted. He hasn't dropped to the ground, because God pours strength in to keep him going.

There are times when you walk, times when you run and times when you soar. In every season it is the strength of God that keeps you walking, running or soaring. Don't despise the season you are in and don't despise other people who are in a different season than you.

I will live strong in my seasons of weakness, for when I am weak then I am strong.

2 Corinthians 12:9-10

"And He said to me, 'My grace is sufficient for you, for My strength is made perfect in weakness.' There- fore most gladly I will rather boast in my infirmities, that the power of Christ may rest upon me. Therefore I take pleasure in infirmities, in reproaches, in needs, in persecutions, in distresses, for Christ's sake. For when I am weak, then I am strong."

Eleanor Roosevelt carried a prayer in her purse: "Our Father, who has set a restlessness in our hearts and made us seekers after that which we can never fully find. Give us a task too hard for us that we may be drawn to You for strength."

Weakness is not an enemy. Weakness is a place to learn the strength of God. Isaiah says we exchange our weakness for His strength. We exchange our limited strength for His powerful strength.

I will live strong because greater is He who is in me than he that is in the world.

1 John 4:4
"You are of God, little children, and have overcome them, because He who is in you is greater than he who is in the world."

Christ is in me. His power is in us. His strength is in us. The Holy Spirit dwells in us and gives us the power and strength we need to overcome the enemies of our soul and the attacks on our lives. No matter how great the enemy, how strong the attack, the Holy Spirit residing in us is greater and stronger.

I will live strong because I know God is for me, not against me.

Romans 8:31
"What then shall we say to these things? If God is for us, who can be against us?"

Psalm 56:9
"When I cry out to You, then my enemies will turn back; This I know, because God is for me."

Elisha had an angry king with an entire army at his disposal coming against him. That's reason to be afraid. One man against an entire nation; the odds aren't too good. Elisha's servant was terrified and was beginning to panic because his master didn't seem very concerned. When he ran to Elisha to let him know that they were doomed, Elisha simply replied, "Those who are with us are more than those who are with them." Then he prayed for the servant to see what Elisha could see in his spirit and the young man saw a mountain full of horses and chariots of fire surrounding them.

Those are the words that need to come from your mouth when life is overwhelming you. "Those who are with us are more than those who are with them." You can be outnumbered and outgunned but never overwhelmed. Open your eyes to see in the Spirit and you will see that the God who lives in you far outguns the armies of enemies that are facing you.

The devil will try to convince you that God isn't for you, that He doesn't care about you, that He's left you alone to deal with these things in your life. Don't forget what Paul says in Romans 8. What will separate you from the love of God? Life? Death? Angels? Principalities? He's got a pretty good list going, but the answer to everything is his simple yet profound declaration: "I am convinced. I have planted my feet on the truth of God's promise and nothing anyone says, nothing anyone does, nothing life throws at me can shake my confidence and trust in His love."

I will live strong because I am more than a conqueror in Christ.

Romans 8:37
"Yet in all these things we are more than conquerors through Him who loved us."

More than conquerors. We don't barely win. We don't scratch out a victory by the skin of our teeth. We more than conquer. We more than overcome. When we finish the race of life, we aren't going to barely slip over the finish line inches ahead of defeat. We are going to blow past the enemy with a power and force that knocks him off his feet. We aren't going to slink past the enemy, hiding in the shadows and hoping he doesn't see us coming. We are running straight at him, face to face, and seeing him go down in defeat.

Don't ask God to help you "get by." Don't pray that you'll be able to hold on until the end. You have Christ in you. Christ doesn't get by. Christ doesn't hold on. He more than conquers.

Numbers 13:30 tells us, "Then Caleb quieted the people before Moses, and said, 'Let us go up at once and take possession, for we are well able to overcome it.'"

1 John 5:4 also refers to a conquering spirit: "For whatever is born of God overcomes the world. And this is the victory that has overcome the world— our faith."

(See also Revelation 2:7, 11, 17, 26; Revelation 3:5, 12, 21; Revelation 21:7; Revelation 12:11.)

I will live strong because I affirm who God is.

God is who He says He is. I am who God says I am. God can do what He says He can do. I can do what God says I can do. God has what He says He has. I have what God says I have. If God says I'm forgiven, I'm forgiven. If God says I'm a victor, I'm a victor. If God says I'm a conqueror, I'm a conqueror. If god says I can overcome that mountain, I can overcome that mountain. If God says He will give me a spirit of faith in trials, I take that spirit of faith.

If God says it, it is true. It doesn't matter what your circumstances are, you have to line up your reality with what God says is reality. Line up your life with the truth of God's Word.

Unshakable Life Declaration #1:
I Will Live Life Strong

I will not faint or be feeble. I will have strength and power greater than average or what is expected. I will be able to stand firm and to sustain any and all attacks. I will endure because I am established and well-fortified in my God.

I Will Love God's House Passionately

I will love God's house with a faithful and fervent spirit and a heart of unwavering devotion, service and zeal.

Psalm 27:4-5
"One thing I have desired of the Lord, that will I seek: that I may dwell in the house of the Lord all the days of my life, to behold the beauty of the Lord, and to inquire in His temple. For in the time of trouble He shall hide me in His pavilion; in the secret place of His tabernacle He shall hide me; He shall set me high upon a rock."

Chapter 4

I Will Love God's House Passionately

*L*oving God and loving God's house are vitally connected and are foundational to fulfilling God's plan and destiny for our life. Every believer must make a choice to serve and love God's house as if they were serving and loving Christ's wife, for that is exactly who the church is.

Before salvation we lived according to our carnal nature. We lived for ourselves, allowing self-will, self-interest, self-desiring, self-pleasing, self-governing attitudes to rule our habits of living. We didn't allow God to be master but lived life according to our own desires.

When we were born again, we put away the old, as 2 Corinthians 5:17 says, "Therefore, if anyone is in Christ, he is a new creation; old things have passed away; behold, all things have become new." Now we are a new person with a new master and live under a new set of principles and convictions. One of those principles is the principle of the house of God.

Independence That Keeps Us from The House of God

An attitude of isolation can separate us from the house of God. It is the attitude that I don't need anyone else, that I can live on my own, independent of relationships. This is an attitude we just reject as it seeks to detach us from the people of God and from the house of God. The enemy of our soul seeks to alienate us from God's house in any way he can. He seeks to shut us out from the fellowship of God's house, cause us to withdraw our heart, affections and become a non-participant, living as an outsider.

Doing life alone is not good. We must intentionally reach out and make close relationships. We must overcome the fear of close friendships and the fear of rejection and become part of His house, part of the Body of Christ.

Martin Luther said it like this, "'Apart from the church, salvation is impossible.' Not that the church provides salvation; God does. But because the 'saved' one can't fulfill what it means to be a Christian apart from the church…"

Faith Declaration

When we recognize his tactics, the battle begins and we become overcomers. We will win the battle. Christ saved us that we might become lovers and builders of His house (Matthew 16:16-18). You are not created to live to yourself, but to live for Christ and His house, the local church (Romans 14:7, 19; Philippians 2:1-2).

This is why we make this unshakable life declaration and live by it: I will love God's house with a faithful and fervent spirit and a heart of unwavering devotion, service and zeal.

Loving God's house passionately is crossing over from attending a church to loving the church. It is crossing over from being a spectator to being a participant. It is crossing over from coming into a building to becoming part of a group of people who are the house of God and being in relationship and commitment with them.

I remember crossing over in my life. I remember changing from casual acquaintances with people in the church to having covenant relationships with them and being burdened and concerned for them. It changed my life and my destiny.

I found my wife in the house of God. I raised my children in the house of God. When I'm in trouble, the house of God comes to my rescue and strengthens and encourages me.

Christ's View of the House of God

Christ is committed to building His house.

In Matthew 16:18-19 Jesus states, "And I also say to you that you are Peter, and on this rock I will build My church, and the gates of Hades shall not prevail against it. And I will give you the keys of the kingdom of heaven, and whatever you bind on earth will be bound in heaven, and whatever you loose on earth will be loosed in heaven."

Christ gave Himself for the church.

In Acts, Paul warns the leaders of the church to carefully "shepherd the church of God which He purchased with His own blood" (Acts 20:28). Christ suffered for His church. He died for her. She is precious to Him and He loves her passionately. Ephesians 5:22-27 compares the husband/wife relationship with that of Christ and the church, commanding husbands to "love your wives, just as Christ also loved the church and gave Himself for her."

Christ dwells in the midst of the church.

Christ is present in the church (Matthew 18:20). He lives there. When believers come together into what we call a church service, Christ is there in the midst of them speaking, moving, touching hearts, changing lives.

Christ is the Head and the church is His body.
Colossians 1:18
> "He is the head of the body, the church, who is the beginning, the firstborn from the dead, that in all things He may have the preeminence."

Christ is the builder of His house called the church.
Hebrews 3:1-6
> "Therefore, holy brethren, partakers of the heavenly calling, consider the Apostle and High Priest of our confession, Christ Jesus, who was faithful to Him who appointed Him, as Moses also was faithful in all His house. For this One has been counted worthy of more glory than Moses, inasmuch as He who built the house has more honor than the house. For every house is built by someone, but He who built all things is God. And Moses indeed was faithful in all His house as a servant, for a testimony of those things which would be spoken afterward, but Christ as a Son over His own house, whose house we are if we hold fast the confidence and the rejoicing of the hope firm to the end."

Loving God's House is a Priority

For David, God's house was a priority. "One thing I have desired of the Lord, that will I seek: that I may dwell in the house of the Lord all the days of my life, to behold the beauty of the Lord and to inquire in His temple" (Psalm 27:4). He loved the house of the Lord (Psalm 26:8), was zealous about the house of the Lord (Psalm 69:9) and had high regard for the house of the Lord (Psalm 84:10).

Do you have a zeal for the house of the Lord? A zeal for God's house to have influence in the culture, a zeal for God's house to minister to people, a zeal for the house of God to change lives?

Lovers of God's house have made a priority value choice.

"One thing have I desired of the Lord..." (Psalm 27:4)

There are many things in life that fight for our attention and our time. There are many things that want our energy. As king, David also had many things encroaching on his life: running the kingdom, taking care of his family, judging court cases. But for David he had a priority value – one thing.

"One thing" is to understand what is first, what is the main thing. It is the most important thing, the thing which comes before anything else. It is the one focus that allows no distractions. One thing is single-mindedness, commitment to the valued choice of the House of God. One thing is a choice we make based on our principles and convictions.

One thing is to value something as being of critical importance. It drives our choices and actions, our priorities and decisions. Jesus loved the church, valued her so much He gave His life for her. The church is important to Christ and it should be important to us.

How do we express value for something? If we value our job, how do we act toward it? If we value our family, how do we treat it? We make time for it. We don't give our family 15 minutes a week and think that's enough. We don't skip work because we'd rather go fishing. We don't show up late to work because we want to sleep in an extra 30 minutes. We value them so we make them a priority in our time. Do you value the house of God? Do you make a priority choice about your time and energy in relationship to the house of God?

Lovers of God's house have made a heart commitment.

"...One thing have I desired..." (Psalm 27:4)

One desire, one passion. David was passionate about God's house. His heart burned within him when he thought about the house of God. He was stirred up about it, excited about it. There was an enthusiasm in him for the house of the Lord. When he brought the ark of the covenant to the tabernacle, the house of God, he didn't order his servants to go get it, then sit and wait for it to show up. He got excited about it. He got involved. He was out dancing in the streets in front of the ark as it was coming.

Be passionate about serving the house of God. David declared, "I would rather be a doorkeeper in the house of my God than dwell in the tents of wickedness" (Psalm 84:10).

There is great honor in serving in the house of the Lord. This doesn't mean being in full-time ministry, although some will serve in that way. Serving the house of God means finding a need and putting your heart into meeting that need. The need may be in the nurseries, with the children's ministry, in being a doorgreeter, stuffing envelopes in the office or mowing the lawn. Every member of the body of Christ is valuable and every member plays a critical part. None is more important than the other. Find your place of service and fill that place passionately. (See also Psalm 84:4; 1 Kings 10:5-8; Psalm 123:2.)

We need to be a functioning part of the church, not bystanders. We need to be participants, not spectators. We need to serve specifically in some area of God's church, to be a giver not a taker, a worker not a relaxer. Serve in God's great house! Look for what you can give, not what you can get!

Lovers of God's house have made a pursuit decision.

"...that will I seek after..." (Psalm 27:4)

Seek means to earnestly search for something with the determination to find it. It isn't a one-time, half-hearted look, but an ongoing pursuit, a persevering and strenuous effort to obtain something. Paul had the same heart of pursuit that David did. "Not that I have already attained, or am already perfected; but I press on, that I may lay hold of that for which Christ Jesus has also laid hold of me. Brethren, I do not count myself to have apprehended; but one thing I do, forgetting those things which are behind and reaching forward to those things which are ahead, I press toward the goal for the prize of the upward call of God in Christ Jesus" (Philippians 3:12-14).

Lovers of God's house have made a placement decision.

"...that I may dwell in the house of the Lord..." (Psalm 27:4)

Dwell means to settle down and make a place your home. It is to be established in a place. A placement decision is a God-decision. It is putting your roots down in a place and being settled there. Being established is to settle in and to begin to form relationships with those around you in the house. A decision to being placed in a house is a decision to commit yourself to the well-being of the house, commit your time, commit your money, commit your passion and vision. The vision of the house becomes your vision. Your life becomes entwined with the lives of those around you in the house.

Ephesians 4:16 says, "from whom the whole body, joined and knit together by what every joint supplies, according to the effective working by which every part does its share, causes growth of the body for the edifying of itself in love." A placement decision is a decision to be joined and knit together, to supply what is needed, to share in doing your part to help the house to grow.

In the Psalms, being placed in the house of the Lord is compared to being planted like a tree. A tree that is planted securely is one that flourishes and has good fruit. Psalm 92:13 states, "Those who are planted in the house of the Lord shall flourish in the courts of our God." Psalm 52:8-9 states, "I am like a green olive tree in the house of God; I trust in the mercy of God forever and ever. I will praise you forever because You have done it; and in the presence of Your saints I will wait on Your name, for it is good." (See also Psalm 23:6; 68:6; 84:4; 91:1; 140:13.)

Chuck Colson said, "When we confess Christ, God's response is to bring us into His church; we become part of His called-out people. When we become followers of Christ, we become members of His church—and our commitment to the church is indistinguishable from our commitment to Him."[1]

Lovers of God's house have made a focus decision.

"…to behold the beauty of the Lord…" (Psalm 27:4)

To behold means to see, to consider, to perceive as the result of reflection or insight. It has the idea of a person acting on what they see. They develop attitudes and make decisions according to what they perceive. Loving God's house is a direct result of making a decision to focus on the beauty of the Lord in the house. The lover of God's house focuses on the beauty of what God is doing, the grace and favor of God on the house.

We see what we look for. If you look for bad, you will find bad. If you look for good, you will find good. No church is perfect. No church is full of perfect people. If you could find a perfect church with perfect people, you and I wouldn't fit in there because we aren't perfect!

Focus on the good things of God in the house of the Lord. Psalm 63:2 says, "So I have looked for You in the sanctuary, to see Your power and Your glory." Psalm 46:8 entreats us to "Come, behold the works of the Lord." (See also Psalm 17:15; 90:17.)

We focus on the good things of God's house by our conversations, words and attitudes. Remember, God calls the church His bride and He died for her. He values her highly and loves her passionately. When you criticize and speak negatively of the house of God, you are criticizing those whom God loves passionately (Psalm 69:9). Be loyal to the house of God. Be loyal to the leaders of His house. Don't sow seeds of discontent or be a troublemaker, gossiping and spreading rumors.

Our attitude toward the house of God is the first level of commitment. We may see its human problems, but our attitude must be that God will use it. We need an expectant attitude that expresses confidence rather than doubt. We must decide to view our church as a body ordained by God for a purpose and believe that He will use it!

Lovers of God's house have made an inquiring decision.

"…to inquire in His temple." (Psalm 27:4)

To inquire means to investigate or meditate on. It is the concept of receiving something and then spending time to meditate and reflect on it. An attitude of inquiry is an attitude of communion with God, expecting Him to reveal the answer needed and give direction, speaking to your heart.

Go to the house of the Lord to inquire, to ask Him to speak to your heart and mind. In the presence of the Lord, He speaks regarding your marriage, your children, your business, your future or whatever is in your heart to seek Him for an answer. David's first response any time he ran into trouble was to inquire of the Lord. Let us follow David's example and go to the house of the Lord with a heart of inquiry.

People Who Loved God's House

Joshua loved God's house and the presence of the Lord.
Exodus 33:11

> "So the Lord spoke to Moses face to face, as a man speaks to his friend. And he would return to the camp, but his servant Joshua the son of Nun, a young man, did not depart from the tabernacle."

David loved God's house.
Psalm 26:8

> "Lord, I have loved the habitation of Your house, and the place where Your glory dwells."

Jesus loved the house of God.
Acts 20:28

> "Therefore take heed to yourselves and to all the flock, among which the Holy Spirit has made you overseers, to shepherd the church of God which He purchased with His own blood."

Ephesians 5:25, 29

> "Husbands, love your wives, just as Christ also loved the church and gave Himself for her... For no one ever hated his own flesh, but nourishes and cherishes it, just as the Lord does the church."

Paul loved the house of God.
Colossians 1:24

> "I now rejoice in my sufferings for you, and fill up in my flesh what is lacking in the afflictions of Christ, for the sake of His body, which is the church."

The Acts 2 People loved the house of God.

Acts 2:46-47

"So continuing daily with one accord in the temple, and breaking bread from house to house, they ate their food with gladness and simplicity of heart, praising God and having favor with all the people. And the Lord added to the church daily those who were being saved."

The Psalms encourage loving God's house.

Psalm 23:6

"Surely goodness and mercy shall follow me all the days of my life; and I will dwell in the house of the Lord forever."

Psalm 26:8

"Lord, I have loved the habitation of Your house, and the place where Your glory dwells."

Psalm 27:4

"One thing I have desired of the Lord, that will I seek: that I may dwell in the house of the Lord all the days of my life, to behold the beauty of the Lord, and to inquire in His temple."

Psalm 36:8

"They are abundantly satisfied with the fullness of Your house, and You give them drink from the river of Your pleasures."

Psalm 42:4

"When I remember these things, I pour out my soul within me. For I used to go with the multitude; I went with them to the house of God, with the voice of joy and praise, with a multitude that kept a pilgrim feast."

Psalm 52:8-9

"But I am like a green olive tree in the house of God; I trust in the mercy of God forever and ever. I will praise You forever, because You have done it; and in the presence of Your saints I will wait on Your name, for it is good."

Psalm 55:14

"We took sweet counsel together, and walked to the house of God in the throng."

Psalm 65:4

"Blessed is the man You choose, and cause to approach You, that he may dwell in Your courts. We shall be satisfied with the goodness of Your house, of Your holy temple."

Psalm 66:13

"I will go into Your house with burnt offerings; I will pay You my vows."

Psalm 69:9

"Because zeal for Your house has eaten me up, and the reproaches of those who reproach You have fallen on me."

Psalm 84:4

"Blessed are those who dwell in Your house; They will still be praising You."

Psalm 84:10

"For a day in Your courts is better than a thousand. I would rather be a doorkeeper in the house of my God than dwell in the tents of wickedness."

Psalm 92:13
> "Those who are planted in the house of the Lord shall flourish in the courts of our God."

Psalm 122:1
> "I was glad when they said to me, 'Let us go into the house of the Lord.'"

Psalm 134:1
> "Behold, bless the Lord, all you servants of the Lord, who by night stand in the house of the Lord!"

The Benefits of Loving God's House

In Psalm 27:5, David rejoices in the benefit of loving God's house, "For in the time of trouble He shall hide me in His pavilion; in the secret place of His tabernacle He shall hide me; He shall set me high upon a rock."

God's house is my hiding place in time of trouble.

To hide is to conceal something to protect it and keep it safe. When trouble comes, God hides us and protects us in His house. Psalm 31: 20 tells us, "You shall hide them in the secret place of Your presence from the plots of man; You shall keep them secretly in a pavilion from the strife of tongues." There is a place of refuge, a place of safety in God. (See also Proverbs 2:7; Psalm 61:4.)

To hide also has the definition of storing something up and treasuring it because of its value. Psalm 31:19 declares, "Oh, how great is Your goodness, which You have laid up for those who fear You, which You have prepared for those who trust in You in the presence of the sons of men!" What does God have stored up or laid up for those who fear Him? His goodness! God brings us to His house where He protects and covers us and pours out on us the goodness He has stored up for us.

God's house is my place to receive strength and stability.

Psalm 27:5 says that He will set me high upon a rock. A rock is a place of stability. It is ground that is firm and solid. A rocky crag is a place where you can get an elevated perspective on the surrounding terrain. If you were in the middle of a wilderness, fleeing from an army, you could climb high upon a rock and find out exactly where your enemy was and which direction to flee for safety.

God is our rock. He gives us an elevated perspective in our time of trouble. In Psalm 73 life tragedies were overwhelming David and nothing made sense. He was discouraged and ready to give up. Then he said, "until I went into the sanctuary of God, then I understood..." (Psalm 73:17). In life there will be situations that slam against our life that we don't understood. They knock us from our feet and shake the ground we stand on. We ask "why" and receive no answer. Some people give up their faith in God when they find themselves in places like this. They quit trusting. They grow bitter and angry at God. But David has an answer. He said, "I went into the sanctuary of God. I went to the house of the Lord."

When life circumstances threaten to undercut your faith, run to the house of God. When unforeseen crises hammer you into the ground, run to His presence. There He will lift you onto a high rock. He will set your feet firmly on Him. He will be your foundation, your rock, your fortress and your shelter. From there you can see with His eyes and His perspective. You may not have the answers you want, but you will cry out the same prayer as Moses, "Go with me and I can go anywhere through anything." You will exclaim the same faith as David,

"Whom have I in heaven but You? And there is none upon earth that I desire besides You. My flesh and my heart fail; But God is the strength of my heart and my portion forever" (Psalm 73:25-26).

When everything around you is being shaken, when there is confusion and questions, find strength in the house of the Lord. Find strength in those who will come around you to bear your burden with you. Find hope and confidence in the presence of God and in the prayers of His body reaching out and holding you firm.

Life Declaration #2:
I Will Love God's House Passionately

I will love God's house with a faithful and fervent spirit and a heart of unwavering devotion, service and zeal.

I Will Hold My Head High

I will boldly declare the greatness of God and the power of His Word. I will not live in defeat, but will stand my ground and fearlessly praise my God. I know God will lift me up and I will live life with my head held high.

Psalm 27:6
"And now my head shall be lifted up above my enemies all around me; Therefore I will offer sacrifices of joy in His tabernacle; I will sing, yes, I will sing praises to the Lord."

Chapter 5

I Will Hold My Head High

The lifting of the head has always been synonymous with victory, expectation, living life above the norm, a happy life attitude. When contenders in any sport win the match, they always lift their heads and their hands to show victory. There is a sense of accomplishment and fulfillment.

The hanging of the head has symbolized discouragement, loss, defeat, bewilderment, grief, sorrow, embarrassment and giving up. Our God is the lifter of our head. Our God lifts our whole life up from the pit, lifting up our mind, will, emotions and spirits.

David had many reasons why he should let his head hang down, his hands fall to his side and despair to overcome him. He had many enemies surrounding him on every side and some enemies on the inside. He was criticized, slandered, and belittled. People sought to hinder his leadership yet he, by God's strength, was able to hold his head high. "And now my head shall be lifted up above my enemies all around me; therefore I will offer sacrifices of joy in His tabernacle; I will sing, yes, I will sing praises to the Lord (Psalm 27:6)." In the face of opposition he refused to yield to defeat but boldly and recklessly proclaimed trust in God.

Now it's your turn. Stop and read the following life declaration out loud with a sense of victory, faith and trust in God. Don't be timid. Read it with force.

> *I will boldly declare the greatness of God and the power of His Word. I will not live in defeat, but will stand my ground and fearlessly praise my God. I know God will lift me up and I will live life with my head held high.*

My Head Lifted High

What does it mean to be lifted up? It means to raise up from the ground or a low place. Someone who is on the ground is someone who is defeated and discouraged. They have been knocked to the ground, beaten, stepped on and crushed. They've given up. God wants to lift that person from the ground and set them back on their feet. He wants to lift them from that low place and set them on high in a new place in God. Psalm 3:3 says, "But You, O Lord, are a shield for me, my glory and the One who lifts up my head."

Being lifted up means to move someone to a new position of rank, power and favor.

God wants to lift the person who has been brought low and place them into a new realm of blessing, a new place of favor with God and man. In Psalm 147:6 it says, "The Lord lifts up the humble."

Being lifted up means to move from a place of defeat to a place of victory.

When a person is in a place of defeat, they think things will never change. They've been defeated. They've been crushed.

Their feet have been knocked out from underneath them and they are at the mercy of the enemy. God comes in to pick them up, dust them off and set them on their feet again. He doesn't leave them at the mercy of the enemy, but He puts fresh strength into them and fresh backbone so they can stand, head high, confident in their God. Proverbs 24:16 says, "A righteous man may fall seven times and rise again." Micah says it even more boldly. "Do not rejoice over me, my enemy. When I fall, I will arise!" (Micah 7:8)

Being lifted up is to move from a limited, tight space to an open and wide space.

Life can box you in and limit you but God comes to push back the boundaries, enlarge the borders and set you in a place of large vision, large dreams, and large possibilities. Habakkuk 3:19 says, "The Lord is my strength. He will make my feet like deer's feet and He will make me walk on my high hills."

Being lifted up is to move from being dispirited to raising the spirit.

A person who has lost spirit is a person who has given up. There is no hope in them, no expectation of success. They have been beaten down until the idea that there is anything other defeat would never cross their mind. To these God declares, "The Lord raises those who are bowed down (Psalm 146:8)." He brings encouragement and hope. He brings fresh strength and fresh perspective.

The Head Pushed Down

Luke 13:11 tells the story of a woman with her head pushed down literally. "There was a woman who had a spirit of infirmity eighteen years, and was bent over and could in no way raise herself up." She had a spirit of infirmity; she was without strength. There was no strength in her, no power, and no ability. In the Greek the phrase "bent over" means that she was completely doubled over and overwhelmed by her lack of strength. There was absolutely nothing she could do to help herself. She was helpless, powerless, completely overcome and without the slightest ounce of strength.

As this woman was pushed down in the physical, there are those who have been pushed down in the spiritual. For years they have had their strength slowly siphoned away by the constant attack of the enemy or the continual burden that they carry. The weight has slowly pushed them down lower and lower, draining their strength until they could not lift their head even if they tried. But there is no trying left in them. There is nothing in them that can begin to hope for change. They are helpless, powerless, completely vulnerable and without the slightest ounce of spiritual strength.

"When Jesus saw her, He called her to Him and said to her, 'Woman, you are loosed from your infirmity.'" (Luke 13:12). You are loosed. You are set free, liberated, no longer a captive. "And He laid His hands on her, and immediately she was made straight" (Luke 13:13). She was made straight. That word straight means perpendicular. She wasn't moved from being completely doubled over to almost doubled over or partially doubled over. She was made perpendicular, straight up and down!

When God lifts your head, He doesn't settle for lifting it enough so you can see past the toes to the knees. He lifts your head straight up so you are standing erect, face to face, unbowed and strong. He puts strength into your back so that, like this woman, you are immediately made straight.

Acts 10:38 says, "God anointed Jesus of Nazareth with the Holy Spirit and with power, who went about doing good and healing all who were oppressed by the devil, for God was with Him."

Jesus came to heal the oppressed. The oppressed are those who are weighed heavily upon, depressed in mind or spirit, crushed and overwhelmed. Jesus came to lift the oppressed, whether the oppression is spiritual, physical, financial, relational or in any other area of life. He came to lift the oppressed, to enable them to stand straight, to be strengthened and to walk victoriously.

Things That Push My Head Down

Troubles push my head down.

Psalm 55:3

"Because of the voice of the enemy, because of the oppression of the wicked; for they bring down trouble upon me, and in wrath they hate me." (See also Psalm 7:16.)

Trouble in the Hebrew is the result of sin. It is the result of sinful acts made against your life and the sorrow and suffering they bring with them.

Iniquities push my head down.

Psalm 38:4

"For my iniquities have gone over my head; Like a heavy burden they are too heavy for me."

Iniquities can be sins for which we have not repented. They become a heavy burden and weigh you down.

Innumerable evils push my head down.

Psalm 40:12

"For innumerable evils have surrounded me; my iniquities have overtaken me, so that I am not able to look up; they are more than the hairs of my head; therefore my heart fails me."

There are evils that surround you. Too many to count, too overwhelming to handle, they press in on you until you cannot lift your eyes past the problems to see God.

Emotional and moral brokenness push my head down.

Isaiah 1:5
"Why should you be stricken again? You will revolt more and more. The whole head is sick, and the whole heart faints."

If you have a weakness in your moral life, it will make your whole way of thinking sick. Your heart will not be right and it will break you down.

Life's overwhelming circumstances push my head down.

Lamentations 3:54
"The waters flowed over my head; I said, 'I am cut off!'" (See also Psalm 30:3)

Your life circumstances have overwhelmed you and you can't handle them. As soon as you get your feet beneath you, they pull you down again. Life, infirmities, weaknesses, doubts, oppressive situations all pull you down into a pit of depression. But God comes to lift you out of the pit.

Discouragement pushes my head down.

Hebrews 12:12
"…strengthen the hands which hang down, and the feeble knees…"

The hands that hang down are hands without strength. You can't do anything. You can't accomplish anything. The discouragement has drained all strength and motivation and the hands quit trying. They give up.

Feeble knees are knees that are paralyzed. There is no strength at all; they are powerless. It's not a lost motivation and discouragement that prevents them from functioning. There is a complete loss of strength.

Personal failure causes discouragement. Someone who is discouraged has been disheartened and depressed. Their confidence has been taken away and they have lost heart. A discouraged person is broken and weak in spirit. Discouragement can be caused by personal failure. You have put your heart into accomplishing something and it didn't work out, resulting in bankruptcy, loss of a business, loss of a relationship, loss of a marriage. Maybe your personal failure is a sin that you can't seem to break free from. It drains your strength, your hope and your confidence in God.

A prolonged battle in spiritual warfare causes discouragement. In Psalm 119:81-82, 86-88, the Psalmist cries out in desperation, "My soul faints for Your salvation, but I hope in Your word. My eyes fail from searching Your word, saying, 'When will You comfort me?' … They persecute me wrongfully; Help me! They almost made an end of me on earth, but I did not forsake Your precepts. Revive me according to Your loving-kindness."

Continual unanswered prayer brings discouragement. Hannah cried out to God for years for a child. She watched as other women bore child after child and yet God seemed to ignore her pleas. She became discouraged and hid in her room crying and not eating. 2 Samuel 1:6 says she was miserable. Proverbs 13:12 says, "Hope deferred makes the heart sick, but when the desire comes, it is a tree of life."

Emotional strain and physical illness can bring discouragement. Sometimes these come from not understanding the contradictions of life. Stephen was stoned and he died; Paul was stoned and he lived. James was beheaded and Peter was released. You try to understand why things happen but life doesn't make sense.

John the Baptist had faithfully obeyed God and preached the good news about the Messiah coming, baptizing those who came to him, and the result of his labor and sacrifice was prison. As he sat in discouragement in his jail cell, he sent a message to Jesus, "Are you the one I've been talking about or has all that I've done been useless?" Jesus sent back a simple answer in Matthew 11:4-6, "Go and tell John the things which you hear and see: the blind see and the lame walk; the lepers are cleansed and the deaf hear; the dead are raised up and the poor have the gospel preached to them. And blessed is he who is not offended because of Me."

Set your eyes on God. Speak to your soul and challenge it to remember who your God is, to remember that He is faithful, and to remember that He is trustworthy.

You can become discouraged and offended with God because you don't understand why things are happening the way they are. He responds with a simple answer, "Remember who I am and what I have done and trust me."

Discouragement comes because of sin. If you have unrepentant sin in your life, you will lose heart and confidence in God. David cried out to God in Psalm 32:3-4, "When I kept silent, my bones grew old through my groaning all the day long. For day and night Your hand was heavy upon me; My vitality was turned into the drought of summer."

As long as David hid his sin, discouragement ate away at him and drained the life from him. But when he confessed his sin to God, he found hope once again. "I acknowledged my sin to You, and my iniquity I have not hidden. I said, 'I will confess my transgressions to the Lord,' and You forgave the iniquity of my sin" (Psalm 32:5).

Discouragement leads into a downward spiral. It can begin with mild discouragement. Perhaps you are just disappointed with God and the way your life is working out. But mild discouragement leads to strong discouragement. Like Elijah, you feel as if the world is against you and you run to hide in the desert, angry at God, angry at people, angry at life. If strong discouragement is not dealt with, it can become disabling, draining your strength and energy and preventing you from functioning. It leads to frustration, the feeling that you are defeated and hopeless. Frustration gives way to depression. Why try because everything you do fails? Your depression feeds itself with vain imaginations, thoughts of how everyone has treated you wrongly and how God has turned his back on you. Those thoughts burn deep into your spirit and you become angry and critical. The critical spirit gives way to resentment and bitterness, which leads to unbelief. You don't believe God and you don't believe His word.

Don't get caught in this downward spiral. Set your eyes on God. Speak to your soul and challenge it to remember who your God is, remember that He is faithful, remember that He is trustworthy. Remember your God.

"Why are you cast down, O my soul? And why are you disquieted within me? Hope in God, for I shall yet praise Him for the help of His countenance. O my God, my soul is cast down within me; Therefore I will remember You from the land of the Jordan, and from the heights of Hermon, from the Hill Mizar" (Psalm 42:4-6). Look at your God and be strengthened. Look to your God and take hope.

The enemy of my soul can push my head down.

Psalm 143:3

"For the enemy has persecuted my soul; He has crushed my life to the ground; He has made me dwell in darkness, like those who have long been dead." (See also Psalm 57:6.)

The enemy comes in to persecute, crush and destroy you. Paul knew this feeling. He said "We are hard-pressed on every side, yet not crushed; we are perplexed, but not in despair." He was hemmed in with troubles from every side, totally surrounded with no way out. Literally, he said, "Troubles are crowding in from every side but we aren't hemmed in. They are forming a hedge tightly around us, but we aren't cramped."

Paul had a divine perspective. When the troubles crowded in so close that he couldn't breathe, he simply lifted his head high and looked down on those troubles from God's perspective and said, "It's really tight, but we aren't trapped. They think they have us cornered, but we've got them right where God wants them—ready to be defeated."

Crises of life can push my head down.

Job 2:13

"So they sat down with him on the ground seven days and seven nights, and no one spoke a word to him, for they saw that his grief was very great."

Crises are those surprises in life, the unexpected things that you weren't ready for. They are the attacks that sneak in the back door and catch you off-guard. Job's attack was so overwhelming that he sat there for one week without speaking. His crisis was so heavy he couldn't talk. He was so burdened and pushed down that he was literally laying on the ground thinking, "I can't handle this."

At the end, Job said, "I had heard of You only by the hearing of the ear, but now my spiritual eye sees You" (Job 42:5, *Amplified*). He saw God for who He was and found fresh hope, new life, resurrected dreams.

When I believe that God is against me, my head is pushed down.

Job 19:10
> "He breaks me down on every side, and I am gone; my hope He has uprooted like a tree."

Before Job reached the point of seeing God, He began to believe the lies of the enemy. He believed that God was against him and that God wasn't going to help him. Never allow yourself to think that God is against you. He won't help you. He doesn't love you. Maybe you don't deserve to be helped, but that doesn't matter because God is a God of mercy and grace. None of us deserve mercy. None of us deserve grace, but God gives it anyway. God has not given up you. He has not stopped loving you. He is not going to walk away from you. Reach out to Him and He will be there.

Failures in my life can push my head down.

Peter experienced failure, complete and total failure. He had promised Jesus he would follow Him and die for Him, even if everyone else left. Instead he denied he even knew Jesus, not just once but three times. He felt as if he had deserted Jesus when Jesus needed him the most. Matthew 26:75 said he "wept bitterly." He cried loudly and with great bitterness and anguish.

This same man that suffered such great failure later writes, "Humble yourselves under the mighty hand of God, that He may exalt you in due time, casting all your care upon Him, for He cares for you" (1 Peter 5:6-7). He will exalt you, He will lift your head up. Peter knew this first-hand. He had been humbled and he had been lifted up. He knew the loving care and grace of God in the midst of his failures and knew he could lift his head high because of the grace and mercy of God.

God is the Lifter of My Head

Psalm 3:3
> "But You, O Lord, are a shield for me, my glory and the One who lifts up my head."

I will hold my head high by setting my eyes on the greatness of God.

Isaiah 40:26
> "Lift up your eyes on high and see who has created these things, who brings out their host by number; He calls them all by name, by the greatness of his might and the strength of His power."

Take your eyes off your problems and off your circumstances and fix them on the greatness of God. The more you stare at your problem, the bigger it gets and the smaller God gets. If your God is too small for your problem, then your God is too small and God is not a small God. He's an awesome God, an all-powerful God. Set your eyes on the greatness of who your God is.

Deuteronomy 10:21
> "He is your praise, and He is your God, who has done for you these great and awesome things which your eyes have seen."

Exodus 15:11
> "Who is like You, O Lord, among the gods? Who is like You, glorious in holiness, fearful in praises, doing wonders?"

Deuteronomy 33:27
> "The eternal God is your refuge, and underneath are the everlasting arms."

I will hold my head high by filling my mouth with the sacrifice of praise.

Lift your head by praising God as David did in Psalm 24:7-9:
> "Lift up your heads, O you gates! And be lifted up, you everlasting doors! And the King of glory shall come in. Who is this King of glory? The Lord strong and mighty, The Lord mighty in battle. Lift up your heads, O you gates! Lift up, you everlasting doors! And the King of glory shall come in."

A song of praise is a response to the presence and power of God. When we worship we are loving the person of the Lord Jesus Christ, the One whom we meet as we praise Him and proclaim Him Lord of all. Worship involves our deepest affections. Worship is the right response to an awareness of God's presence

Sometimes it is hard to praise God; that is when we give a sacrifice of praise. A sacrifice of praise is a sacrifice of worship from a heart of faith; it is worship given in the darkest hour of life in the midst of circumstances you can't understand. A sacrifice of praise is worship given from a broken heart. "For You do not desire sacrifice, or else I would give it; you do not delight in burnt offering. The sacrifices of God are a broken spirit, a broken and a contrite heart; these, O God, You will not despise" (Psalm 51:16-17). (See also Hebrews 13:15.)

Jonah had rebelled against God and ended up in the belly of a fish at the bottom of the ocean. He responded in prayer and cried out to God, "Out of the belly of Sheol I cried, and You heard my voice.... When my soul fainted within me, I remembered the Lord; and my prayer went up to You, into

Your holy temple. But I will sacrifice to You with the voice of thanksgiving; I will pay what I have vowed. Salvation is of the Lord" (Jonah 2:1-2, 7, 9).

Paul and Silas had done nothing wrong. They were obeying God and preaching the gospel and it landed them in jail, after they had been beaten. There was no reason to worship God. He had let them get thrown into that awful place. But they lifted up their voices in a sacrifice of praise and Acts 16:25-26 says, "At midnight Paul and Silas were praying and singing hymns to God, and the prisoners were listening to them. Suddenly there was a great earthquake, so that the foundations of the prison were shaken; and immediately all the doors were opened and everyone's chains were loosed." A sacrifice of praise shakes the gates of hell and looses the hand of God.

I will hold my head high by the lifting power of the Holy Spirit.

Romans 15:13 says, "Now may the God of hope fill you with all joy and peace in believing, that you may abound in hope by the power of the Holy Spirit." (See also Ezekiel 3:12; 43:5.) Be filled with the Holy Spirit. This isn't a one-time event, but an ongoing relationship. Be filled with the Holy Spirit. Pray in the Holy Spirit.

In Psalm 51:11-12, the Psalmist prays, "Do not cast me away from Your presence, and do not take Your Holy Spirit from me. Restore to me the joy of Your salvation, and uphold me by Your generous Spirit." Uphold me, sustain me, and strengthen me through your Spirit.

Andrew Murray said, "We need a period daily for secret fellowship. Time to turn from daily occupation and search our hearts in His presence. Time to study His Word with reverence and godly fear. Time to seek His face and ask Him to make Himself known to us. Time to wait until we know that He sees and hears us so that we can make our wants known to Him in words that come from the depth of our hearts. Time to let God deal with our special needs, to let His light shine in our hearts, to let ourselves be filled with His Spirit!"[1]

Shut yourself apart with God, away from other people and distractions. Develop a one-on-one relationship with God, you and Him. Allow the Holy Spirit to come in and fill you, lifting your head, changing your perspective, bringing fresh strength and power.

I will hold my head high by filling my mouth with the Word of God.

Psalms 119:28

"My soul melts from heaviness; strengthen me according to Your word." (See also Psalm 119:9, 11, 16, 50, 105.)

The soul is in an intense battle and is melting away in the trickling down of the tears. It is overwhelmed with life, without hope and without any future, but they find strength and hope in the Word of God.

"You need time to feed upon the Word of God, and to draw from it life for your soul. Through His Word, His thoughts and His grace enter our hearts and lives. Take time each day to read the Bible, even if it be only a few verses; meditate upon what you have read, and thus assimilate the bread of life. If you do not take the trouble to let God speak to you through His Word, how can you expect to be led by the Spirit?"[2]

I will hold my head high by standing my ground and fighting back.

1 Timothy 6:12

"Fight the good fight of faith, lay hold on eternal life, to which you were also called and have confessed the good confession in the presence of many witnesses." (See also Ephesians 6:10.)

We must quit running from the devil, his lies, his attacks and his oppression. If we give up, he will keep backing us up and moving against us. We must become aggressive, initiate forceful action, be energetic and boldly assertive. "Defeat doesn't finish a man—quit does. A man is not finished when he's defeated. He's finished when he quits."[3] Don't quit. Don't give up. Stand your ground and lift your head!

In 2 Chronicles 20, Judah was under attack by three nations who had joined together to destroy them: "We have no power against this great multitude that is coming against us; nor do we know what to do…" (2 Chronicles 20:12). He did not have the resources or the ability to stand against the army coming against him. The destruction of the nation was certain and Jehoshaphat had no idea of what to do next, but he didn't finish his prayer there. "We have no power against this great multitude that is coming against us; nor do we know what to do, but our eyes are upon You."

No matter what circumstances are facing you, what trials and tribulations are coming against you, they can't change who God is. He is still God. He is still faithful. His mercy and compassion are still there for you.

When the challenge is beyond your strength, lift your head and set your eyes on your God. Look to Him. When Jehoshaphat and his army set their eyes on God, the word of the Lord came and said, "Do not be afraid nor dismayed because of this great multitude, for the battle is not yours, but God's… You will not need to fight in this battle. Position yourselves, stand still and see the salvation of the Lord, who is with you" (2 Chronicles 20:15, 17). God will fight for you. He will be with you. You lift your head, set your eyes on Him, position yourselves in obedience to Him and watch to see what He will do.

Jehoshaphat and the people positioned themselves for battle. Those he positioned in the forefront were the worshippers. 2 Chronicles 20:21 says, "He appointed those who should sing to the Lord, and who should praise the beauty of holiness, as they went out before the army and were saying: 'Praise the Lord, for His mercy endures forever.'"

What do you do when you are facing certain defeat? What do you do when the circumstances arrayed against you are overwhelming and beyond your ability to handle? What do you do when you are powerless and when you don't have the wisdom to deal with the situation?

Set your eyes on God. Lift your head and look to Him. Position yourself in obedience to Him and begin to worship. Begin to offer the sacrifice of praise and exult in your God whose mercy toward you never runs out.

I will hold my head high believing God is in charge of my seasons.

Lamentations 3:22-23
"Through the Lord's mercies we are not consumed, because His compassions fail not. They are new every morning; great is Your faithfulness." (See also Galatians 6:9; Genesis 8:22.)

When Job lost everything, his wife told him to curse God and die. His friends told him he was a sinner and deserved everything that had happened to him. But Job had an amazing understanding of the sovereignty of God. "Naked I came from my mother's womb, and naked shall I return there. The Lord gave, and the lord has taken away; blessed be the name of the Lord" (Job 1:21). He knew that the good and bad in the seasons of His life were all in God's hands. It didn't matter if he understood why things were happening; he trusted His God.

Whatever you are going through, whatever season of life you are in, God is in charge. He is there. God was in Job's season although Job couldn't see it until the end. God is in your season even if you can't see it. Put your trust in Him. Set your hope and your faith on Him. No matter what circumstances are facing you, what trials and tribulations are coming against you, they can't change who God is. He is still God. He is still faithful. His mercy and compassion are still there for you.

The Power to Live Life with Your Head Held High

Kathryn Kuhlman once said, "The Holy Spirit is the secret of the power in my life. All I have to do is surrender my life to Him."[4] The power to live life with your head held high only comes through the power of God working in your life.

Paul says in Romans 1:16, "I am not ashamed of the gospel of Christ, for it is the power of God to salvation for everyone who believes..." He reinforces this in 1 Corinthians 1:18: "For the message of the Christ is foolishness to those who are perishing, but to us who are being saved it is the power of God."

Partner with the Holy Spirit.

In Ephesians 3:16, Paul prays, "that from his glorious, unlimited resources he will give you mighty inner strength through his Holy Spirit" (*New Living Translation*). God has an unlimited resource of power. His power is not limited and that is the power which He makes available to us through the Holy Spirit. As Kathryn Kuhlman said, that power comes through the simple principle of surrendering your life to Him, allowing Him to be the Lord of your life.

Order your heart to align with faith.

Do you believe God is a good God, an "all things are possible" God? Do you believe He is all-powerful, at all times, and in every circumstance? Do you believe that He is a God who is able to do anything? Wonderful! I'm so glad you believe that! The real question to answer now is, do you live as though those things are true? We give voice to the truths of God's word verbally, but the difficulty is living those truths.

Let's look at Hebrews 11. It says by faith Abel offered. By faith Noah prepared. By faith Abraham obeyed. By faith Abraham dwelt. By faith Sarah received. By faith Isaac blessed. By faith Jacob worshiped. By faith Joseph gave instructions. Do you see a pattern? Each time the author says, "by faith" it is followed by a verb. Every time faith is expressed, it is expressed in action.

James 2:20-22 states it this way, "But do you want to know, O foolish man, that faith without works is dead? Was not Abraham our father justified by works when he offered Isaac his son on the altar? Do you see that faith was working together with his works, and by works faith was made perfect?"

Alignment means to bring something into correct position in relationship to something else. You must align your life with your faith, align your action with your faith. If you believe something, your life must demonstrate it. Do you believe that God is great? Live like it. Do you believe in the power of God's Word in your life? Demonstrate it. Do you believe that God will lift you up? Then lift your head high and act like it.

War against destructive thoughts and habits.

Your thoughts are your biggest adversary in aligning your life in faith with the Word of God. 2 Corinthians 10:5 tells us to "pull down every proud obstacle that is raised against the knowledge of God; we take every thought captive and make it obey Christ" (*Today's English Version*).

Pulling down is not a passive activity. Pulling down means to grab those thoughts and force them to come into submission. "We take every thought captive" is a warfare term. It means to gain complete control over someone through force and take them prisoner. You need to aggressively go to war against those thoughts. Force them to align with the Word of God. Don't just push them into a corner and ignore them. Take them into complete control, utterly demolish them. Through God's power you can do it.

Exchange your weakness for Christ's strength.

Exchange means to put one thing in the place of another. Put Christ's strength in the place of your weakness. Isaiah 40:29 promises, "He gives power to the weak and to those who have no might He increases strength." In Hebrews 11:34 the author tells of those who by faith "out of weakness were made strong, became valiant in battle, turned to flight the armies of the aliens."

Remember, it is through the power of the Holy Spirit, through exchanging your weakness for His strength, that you can align your heart with faith and bring your thoughts into captivity. It's not your power; it is His.

Replenish daily through prayer and the Word.

David cries out in Psalm 119:25, "My soul clings to the dust; revive me according to Your word." Isaiah echoes this cry in 57:15, "For thus says the High and Lofty One who inhabits eternity, whose name is Holy: 'I dwell in the high and holy place, with him who has a contrite and humble spirit, to revive the spirit of the humble, and to revive the heart of the contrite ones.'"

Andrew Murray challenges us to seek God fervently: "We need a period daily for secret fellowship. Time to turn from daily occupation and search our hearts in His presence. Time to study His Word with reverence and godly fear. Time to seek His face and ask Him to make Himself known to us. Time to wait until we know that He sees and hears us so that we can make our wants known to Him in words that come from the depth of our hearts. Time to let God deal with our special needs, to let His light shine in our hearts, to let ourselves be filled with His Spirit!"[5]

Life Declaration #3:
I Will Hold My Head High

I will boldly declare the greatness of God and the power of His Word. I will not live in defeat, but will stand my ground and fearlessly praise my God. I know God will lift me up and I will live life with my head held high.

I Will Have an Overflowing Heart

I will fill my heart with God's Word, prayer and praise. For out of my heart overflow, the inner voice of God is heard clearly, powerfully and distinctly.

Psalm 27:7-8
"Hear, O Lord, when I cry with my voice! Have mercy also upon me, and answer me. When You said, 'Seek My face,' my heart said to You, 'Your face, Lord, I will seek.'"

Chapter 6

I Will Have an Overflowing Heart

When we are facing life struggles and shakings, we look for answers. We want explanations and solutions. We want to understand why and to find a way of escape. David's response was to seek God, "Hear, O Lord, when I cry with my voice! Have mercy also upon me, and answer me. When You said, 'Seek my face,' my heart said to You, 'Your face, Lord, I will seek'"(Psalm 27:7-8). He had a heart that aligned with the voice of God, a heart to hear and obey. When God spoke, David's heart immediately responded in obedience.

There are many voices in life that try to get our attention, many voices that seek to shape our life and destiny. Friends, family, coworkers, employers, teachers all speak up loudly and persistently, urging us to listen to their opinions and do things their way. But the most important voice in our lives is the voice of God that speaks loudly and clearly in our hearts. The voice of God is heard most distinctly when our hearts are overflowing with the Holy Spirit, overflowing with the things of God.

Faith Declaration

I will fill my heart with God's Word, prayer and praise. For out of the overflow of my heart, the inner voice of God is heard clearly, powerfully and distinctly.

What Is in Your Heart?

The things that flow out of your heart shape your life, form your boundaries, and define who you are. Your mouth will speak what is in your heart. You may try to hide what is deep inside, but your heart will be exposed. Luke 6:45 tells us, "A good man out of the good treasure of his heart brings forth good; and an evil man out of the evil treasure of his heart brings forth evil. For out of the abundance of the heart his mouth speaks."

What is the abundance in your heart? What is your heart filled with? Your heart can be filled with your own ways (Proverbs 14:14). Your heart can be filled with lies (Acts 5:3). What does your heart say when difficult times come? What does your heart do when God speaks? Does it respond to Him?

I challenge you to begin to fill your heart with the word of God until the word of God flows out of you. Align your heart with the Word so that its immediate response in any situation is to agree with God.

God Wants to Speak to You

You have the voice of God in your life. He speaks to your heart. He also speaks through other ways to confirm His word, such as wise counsel, prophecy, preaching, etc. But the voice of God must start in your heart. If it does not start in your heart, you have no foundation for the word to take root. The pivotal points in my life were not great counsel, prophetic words, but they were the voice of God speaking quietly into my heart, a few words, a God-thought. They were confirmed later through other ways, but they began with the small, still voice of God in my heart.

A.W. Tozer describes "thirsty hearts whose longings have been wakened by the touch of God within them."[1] I want the longings of your heart to be awakened so that you will know, "God spoke to me." I want your heart to be touched by God so that from the overflow will come a clear voice of God to your life.

God is speaking.

God wants to speak to His people. Since Adam and Eve He has tried to talk to them, to have a relationship with them. In the Bible He spoke through creation, angels, prophets, dreams, visions, and casting lots (Urim and Thummin). He spoke with a gentle voice, with fire, in a burning bush, through preaching, through symbolic acts, signs, miracles, and writing on the wall. He spoke through prayer, through impressions, through quickened scriptures, through people, through circumstances, and through the Holy Spirit. He is not passive about speaking to His people (John 10:27).

God wants you to know His thoughts toward you.

God wants to speak to you His thoughts about you. He has unique and specific thoughts designed just for you, for a specific time and a specific purpose. He wants to communicate directly to you concerning your needs, your questions about the future and decisions you are making now.

God desires to speak to you a "now word" for a "now time" so that you can know and understand His plans and designs for your life. He wants to reveal His thoughts toward you to encourage you, inspire you and cause you to hit the mark that He has set for you. Jeremiah 29:11-12 says, "'For I know the thoughts that I think toward you', says the Lord, 'thoughts of peace and not of evil, to give you a future and a hope.'" (See also Psalm 85:8.)

Your thoughts are so far below God's thoughts that no matter how carefully you plan and think about your life, your ideas are far inferior to God's plans for your life. You can strategize and set goals, but God's plans are vastly superior to your ways and your thoughts. Isaiah 55:8-9 says, "'My thoughts are not your thoughts, nor are your ways My ways,' says the Lord. 'For as the heavens are higher than the earth, so are My ways higher than your ways, and My thoughts than your thoughts.'" God desires to reveal His thoughts because your human thinking is inferior to God's best. Ephesians 3:20 says, "Now to Him who is able to do exceedingly abundantly above all that we ask or think, according to the power that works in us..."

Psalms 139:17 declares, "How precious also are Your thoughts to me, O God! How great is the sum of them!" In *The Message Bible*: "Your thoughts—how rare, how beautiful! God, I'll never comprehend them!" *The Amplified Bible* states it like this: "How precious and weighty also are Your thoughts to me, O God! How vast is the sum of them!" The *New Living Bible* marvels, "How precious are your thoughts about me, O God! They are innumerable!"

God's thoughts toward you are vast and innumerable. His intentions for your life are great. His purposes for you are beautiful and incomprehensible. His designs for you are rare and precious.

Begin to fill your heart with the Word of God and begin to listen carefully to the voice of God in your life. Listen diligently to what He has to say, wait patiently before Him and be passionate about walking in obedience to what He says.

Discern the Thoughts Toward You

There are thoughts in motion toward you from your own limited or carnal mind.

In Romans 8:7, Pauls says, "Because the carnal mind is enmity against God; for it is not subject to the law of God, nor indeed can be." (See also Romans 7:14)

Your carnal mind is limited in its thinking. It will never grasp the wonder of God's thoughts toward you because it is at odds with God's thoughts. It sees only itself. It is self-willed, self-focused and self-seeking.

There are thoughts in motion toward you from your past ruts of negative thinking.

2 Corinthians 10:4-6 tells us, "For the weapons of our warfare are not carnal but mighty in God for pulling down strongholds, casting down arguments and every high thing that exalts itself against the knowledge of God, bringing every thought into captivity to the obedience of Christ, and being ready to punish all disobedience when your obedience is fulfilled."

You have formed thinking habits that affect how you perceive things. Maybe they are thoughts of failure, thoughts that nothing ever works so why try. Perhaps they are thoughts of rejection and negativity. Maybe your thoughts are thoughts of pride, that you don't deserve to be treated in a certain manner, that you deserve better things from life than you are getting.

You form patterns of thinking and these will hinder you from hearing God's thoughts for you. Take 2 Corinthians 10:4-6 to heart and bring every thought captive to obeying Christ. A thought may seem to be a good thought, but if it is not in obedience to Christ and exalting God, it's a wrong thought.

There are thoughts in motion toward you from the enemy of your soul, the devil.

Ephesians 6:12 describes our enemies: "For we do not wrestle against flesh and blood, but against principalities, against powers, against the rulers of the darkness of this age,

against spiritual hosts of wickedness in the heavenly places."
(See also Ephesians 6:16-17.)

When Jesus was tempted by the devil in the wilderness,
the devil had thoughts for Him. They didn't sound that bad
at first. Jesus was hungry and He could make the stones to be
bread. Is that wrong? If He jumped from the top of the temple,
it would be a great sign to everyone who was watching and
demonstrate that He was the Son of God. They don't sound
like bad thoughts, but they were not God-thoughts.

Jesus responded quickly with the written thoughts of
God in Matthew 4:4, "But He answered and said, 'It is written…'" He chose the thoughts of God over the thoughts of the
enemy.

The devil will lie to you. A lie is something that is presented
to give you a wrong impression. Sometimes it is true facts, but
communicated in a way that will deceive and give a false image.
Sometimes a lie is something that is completely false with no
truth in it at all. A lie is a broken promise, an empty promise.
It is meant to deceive and lead someone astray.

Don't allow the culture to determine
who you can be in God. Culture may
tell you that you are so intelligent you
must pursue a career in science or
medicine, but if God has spoken to you
about missions, listen to God's voice.

What kind of lies does the devil tell us? You are not forgiven. You are never going to succeed at anything. You can
never change so don't try. Your past has cancelled God's future
for you. God may bless and use other people, but not you. You
have no destiny, no purpose. You have many weaknesses that

make you inferior to most everyone else. You can live however you want and still be blessed by God. You can secretly sin and no one will ever know.

What kind of lies do other people tell us? You are too spiritual. Why don't you just enjoy life and be normal? You are too ambitious. You are always serving and doing things for the church and leadership. You spend too much time in church. Are you in some kind of cult? You should do what you want with your life. You should set your own standards. Don't let the legalistic, out-of-touch-with-reality church do it.

Psalm 120:2 offers a prayer of release from lies: "Deliver my soul, O Lord, from lying lips and from a deceitful tongue."

There are thoughts in motion toward you from the people around you with limited knowledge.

In 1 Samuel, David went down to the war zone where his father sent him to take food to his brothers. When he heard Goliath taunting the Israelites, righteous indignation rose up inside him and he asked, "Who is this pagan Philistine, that he is allowed to defy the armies of the living God?" (1 Samuel 17:26, *New Living Translation*)

When his older brother heard this, he began furious with David and accused him of shirking his responsibilities with the sheep to come gawk at the battle. The brother had limited knowledge. He accused David of something that was untrue because David had come in obedience to his father.

When David decided to go against Goliath, Saul had thoughts toward him as well. He said, "You are not able to go against this Philistine to fight with him; for you are a youth, and he a man of war from his youth" (1 Samuel 17:33). Saul was limiting David, judging him by his own perception. But David was seeing himself through God's eyes. He knew that the God He served was perfectly capable of taking on a giant, even through a shepherd boy. David heard God's thoughts more clearly than he heard Saul's thoughts.

What thoughts are you hearing? What are people saying to you and about you? Don't allow other people's perceptions to limit what God has said to you. If God has told you to do something, you must obey. There is a wise balance to this in that in the multitude of counselors there is wisdom and confirmation to the voice of God. That is why God has put parents, pastors and wise leaders into your life.

There may be seasons when you will have to do as Mary did: take the word that God has given you and hide it in your heart until God brings it to pass. Mary, the mother of Jesus, didn't shout from the rooftops what God had spoken to her. She took the prophetic words and pondered them, meditated on them, prayed about them and waited for God to fulfill them. When He did, she was ready because she was waiting and prepared.

There are thoughts in motion toward you from your world culture, which may be twisted and wrong.

Romans 12:1-2 says, "I beseech you therefore, brethren, by the mercies of God, that you present your bodies a living sacrifice, holy, acceptable to God, which is your reasonable service. And do not be conformed to this world, but be transformed by the renewing of your mind, that you may prove what is that good and acceptable and perfect will of God."

Don't allow the culture to determine who you can be in God. Culture may tell you that you are so intelligent you must pursue a career in science or medicine, but God has spoken to you about missions. Perhaps working with alcoholics is not as glamorous as working with politicians. Perhaps being a doctor in a prominent hospital is not as successful as being a doctor in a small country town. God has called you to be a wise steward of the talent and giftings that He has placed in you. A wise steward uses those talents for the purpose that the Master has designed them, regardless of the world's opinion.

There are thoughts in motion toward you from God through the Holy Spirit, the written word of God and the quickened word of God.

➤ "I have your life written out in My book. I have plans for you, even before you were born. I have had you in My heart always."

➤ "I have forgiven you of all your past and removed your sins as far as the east is from the west."

➤ "I have destined for you to be a blessed person, to live an abundant life, to receive great things from Me."

➤ "I have given you a dream, a vision, a hope. You are to live your life with your head lifted high for you are Mine."

➤ "I love you the way you are and I love you too much to let you stay the way you are. I am changing you for your good."

The Power of an Overflowing Heart

The heart is the inner spiritual man inside each person who is born again. It has spiritual senses and can see, hear, feel and know in the spirit. When you are born again, you begin to perceive things differently than someone who does not know

God. You see things differently, feel things differently, and hear things differently. You begin to make decisions based on the things you feel, hear and see.

Ephesians 1:17-18 tells us that your inner man has the ability to hear God. "That the God of our Lord Jesus Christ, the Father of glory, may give to you the spirit of wisdom and revelation in the knowledge of Him, the eyes of your understanding being enlightened; that you may know what is the hope of His calling, what are the riches of the glory of His inheritance in the saints." Your inner man needs to be filled with an expectation of hearing the voice of God.

An overflowing heart is one that is so full of the Word of God that it gushes out, floods, overwhelms. An overflow occurs when there is so much of something that it cannot be contained. That is the desire of our heart – to be so filled with God, so filled with His word, that we cannot contain it. It pours out of our life in an ongoing, continuous flood.

The overflowing heart is the source of our life.

Proverbs 4:23 advises us to "Keep your heart with all diligence, for out of it spring the issues of life."

A spring is the source of a river, the place where the river begins, the starting point of the flow. If a spring has good water, the water that flows into the river will be good. If a spring has contaminated water, the river will be contaminated as well.

The same thing is true in your life. Your heart is the starting point of everything in your life. Whatever the starting point looks like, the river will become. If the starting point of your heart is rooted in God, the Word, purity, everything in your life will reflect that flow. If your heart is filled with the Word, your life will be filled with the Word. If your heart is filled with bitterness, resentment or anger, so is your life.

Jesus said it this way in Luke 6:43-45, "For a good tree does not bear bad fruit, nor does a bad tree bear good fruit.

For every tree is known by its own fruit. For men do not gather figs from thorns, nor do they gather grapes from a bramble bush. A good man out of the good treasure of his heart brings forth good; and an evil man out of the evil treasure of his heart brings forth evil. For out of the abundance of the heart his mouth speaks."

Guard the spring. Guard the starting point. Once it begins to flow, it will define everything about you. It becomes the source of your life.

The overflowing heart pours out in an abundance.

Matthew 12:34 says, "For out of the abundance of the heart the mouth speaks."

Abundance is the surplus, what is on top. The abundance will come out no matter how badly you try to hide it.

If your heart is full of grace, grace will flow out of your life. If your heart is full of jealousy, jealousy will flow out of your life. You can't hide what's inside. "For out of the abundance of the heart the mouth speaks." What is abundant in your heart? What overflows out of your heart? Do you have a little bit of the Word but an abundance of pride?

During the California gold rush, crooked miners would try to sell a worthless mine by salting it. They would go to extreme measures to give the appearance of a valuable gold mine, even digging through six feet of earth in order to plant some gold ore and then covering it up. When the buyer came to evaluate the claim, he would find gold and buy the mine. The problem was there wasn't an abundance of gold. There wasn't an overflow. There was only the gold that was planted there to give an appearance of riches.

You can try to give an appearance of God in your heart, paint gold veneer on some rocks and make it look good, but the Bible says that out of the abundance the mouth will speak.

The salted claim will give way to the truth, the gold veneer will flake off and the abundance of the heart will be clearly seen.

The overflowing heart has a treasure.

Luke 6:45 tells us, "A good man out of the good treasure of his heart brings forth good; and an evil man out of the evil treasure of his heart brings forth evil. For out of the abundance of the heart his mouth speaks."

A treasure is something deposited into your life. It is something that is valuable and highly prized. What do you deposit into your life? When life throws things at you, which things do you keep and hide in your heart and which do you let go of? When someone treats you wrong, do you deposit forgiveness or resentment in your heart? When your dreams are crushed, do you deposit disappointment or trust in God? Life does not deposit things into your heart. Your response to life does.

The overflowing heart flows.

In John 7:38, Jesus says, "He who believes in Me, as the Scripture has said, out of his heart will flow rivers of living water."

A flow is not something that starts and stops. It isn't a hit-and-miss. Some days the river flows and some days it doesn't. I don't look out my office window to the Columbia River and wonder, "Will it be flowing today?" It's a continuous act. It keeps flowing. An overflowing heart pours out consistently.

The overflowing heart has a theme.

In Psalms 45:1, David says, "My heart is overflowing with a good theme."

Your heart overflows with a theme that marks your life. What is your theme for your life? When people are asked to describe you, what one word would they say?

He is a giver. In every situation in life, he is always giving to people. She is a servant. Whenever there is a need, she is there to serve and meet that need. He is kind. You never hear him speak badly about anyone. He is always speaking words of encouragement and blessing to people. She is negative. She's always criticizing people, seeing the worst in them, speaking negatively about them.

What is your theme? Loyalty, selfishness, dependability, indecisiveness, love? Your theme reveals your overflow because your overflow defines who you are. Whatever your heart is overflowing with marks your life and identifies you.

The Overflowing Heart Encourages a Praying Heart

The overflowing heart cries out to God.

In Psalm 27:7, David calls out to God: "Hear, O Lord, when I cry with my voice!..."

An overflowing heart cries out to God. It calls out in earnest and insistent pleading. An overflowing heart is persistent in voicing its need for God. The overflowing heart understands that its sufficiency, its strength, is found only in relationship with God.

The overflowing heart cries out, "Whom have I in heaven but You? And there is none upon earth that I desire besides You. My flesh and my heart fail; but God is the strength of my heart and my portion forever" (Psalm 73:25-26). The life of the overflowing heart, the strength and passion of the overflowing heart, is the presence of God.

Oswald Chambers said, "If in the first waking moment of the day you learn to fling the door back and let God in, every public thing will be stamped with the presence of God."[2]

The overflowing heart believes it will receive answers.

Psalm 27:7 says, "…have mercy also upon me, and answer me…"

An overflowing heart comes with the simple childlike expectancy that the Heavenly Father loves and cares and is listening to each prayer. It believes Psalm 91:15: "He shall call upon Me, and I will answer him; I will be with him in trouble; I will deliver him and honor him." The overflowing heart understands that "He desires to be more present to us than we are to seek Him. He desires to give Himself to us more readily than we are to receive Him."[3]

God promises, "Call to Me, and I will answer you, and show you great and mighty things, which you do not know" (Jeremiah 33:3). The overflowing heart cries out, "In the day of my trouble I will call upon You, for You will answer me" (Psalm 86:7). and God responds, "He shall call upon Me, and I will answer him; I will be with him in trouble" (Psalm 91:15).

The overflowing heart hears the voice of God in the heart.

Psalm 27:8 describes the heart's response to God: "When You said, 'seek My face,' my heart said to You, 'Your face, Lord, I will seek.'"

We need to learn to quiet our hearts to hear the voice of God. C.S. Lewis observed:

> "The real problem of the Christian life comes where people usually do not look for it. It comes the very moment you wake up each morning. All your wishes and hopes for the day are rushed at you like wild animals and the first job each morning consists simply in shoving them all back and listening to that other voice, taking that other point of view, letting that other larger, stronger, quieter life come flowing in and so on all day."[4]

Learn to quiet your heart before the Lord. Many things clamor for your heart. Many voices cry out for your attention, but you need to learn to be still, to silence the other voices and listen for the only voice that matters – the voice of God. You have to take control of your mind and not allow the worries and concerns and thoughts about the day to push in. (See also Psalm 46:10; 4: 4; 23:2; Isaiah 30:15.)

Learn how to sit before the Lord. In 2 Samuel 7:18, "King David went in and sat before the Lord..." He didn't bring his prayer list and request, he just came and sat before the Lord. He meditated on the Word of God and listened. This takes time. Our culture is a fast-food culture. We want everything right away; we don't want to wait for anything. But we must learn to sit quietly in the presence of God, to listen to His voice. We need to learn as David did in Psalm 62:5: "My soul, wait silently for God alone, for my expectation is from Him." Don't listen for what other people think. Listen for God. Expect Him to speak.

Find a solitary place alone with God. Follow Jesus' example of Mark 1:35. "Now in the morning, having risen a long while before daylight, He went out and departed to a solitary place; and there he prayed." This is a place of seclusion, a shutting out of all other voices and sitting in silence, allowing God to speak to your heart clearly and positively, with an unmistakable voice. He will move in your spirit and impress your mind.

Andrew Murray said, "'When you pray,' says Jesus, 'enter into your inner chamber, and having shut the door, pray to your Father which is in secret.' That means two things. Shut the world out, withdraw from all worldly thoughts and occupations, and shut yourself in alone with God, to pray to Him in secret. Let this be your chief object in prayer, to realize the presence of your heavenly Father. Let your watchword be: Alone with God."[5]

Develop a one-on-one relationship with God, you and Him, not you and everyone else and God. Don't depend on someone else to hear from God for you. Hear what He has to say to you yourself. Shut the door, shut out all distracting voices and tune in your heart to the one voice that you long to hear.

Learn to hear the still small voice of God. Elijah was desperate to hear from God. He was discouraged, depressed and feeling sorry for himself. In 1 Kings 19:11-13 God told him, "'Go out, and stand on the mountain before the Lord.' And behold, the Lord passed by, and a great and strong wind tore into the mountains and broke the rocks in pieces before the Lord, but the Lord was not in the wind; and after the wind an earthquake, but the Lord was not in the earthquake; and after the earthquake a fire, but the Lord was not in the fire; and after the fire a still small voice. So it was, when Elijah heard it, that he wrapped his face in his mantle and went out and stood in the entrance of the cave. Suddenly a voice came to him, and said, 'What are you doing here, Elijah?'"

In that quiet moment, Elijah heard a pivotal word and reached a turning point in his life and ministry.

Learn to listen to the still small voice of the Holy Spirit. Listen for the voice that speaks in the quietness of your heart. Listen for the whisper of God. To hear the whisper, you have to get close to God, to lean in close to Him in a place of intimacy.

The overflowing heart responds with intercessory prayer.

Psalm 27:8 says, "…Your face, Lord, I will seek."

To seek is to earnestly look for, hunt after, search out something. It isn't a half-hearted response, but a whole-hearted pursuing after God. Deuteronomy 4:29 says, "You will find Him if you seek Him with all your heart and with all your soul." Seeking God isn't a casual hobby. It's not something you do whenever you have the time. It requires all your heart, your complete heart, nothing held back. It takes everything that is in you, every dream, every desire, every passion. It takes all that you hold and value laid out on the altar and given to Him as you seek after Him.

Seeking God is a deliberate decision. 1 Chronicles 22:19 says, "Now set your heart and your soul to seek the Lord your God." It is a purposeful decision, a determined passion. You are determined. You make time. You make this a priority. (See also Psalm 24:6; 69:32; Isaiah 55:6; Jeremiah 29:13; Daniel 9:3; Matthew 7:7; Hebrews 11:6.)

The Overflowing Heart Faith Declarations

I will cleanse my heart from all the unnecessary clutter.

Psalm 51:2,7
> "Wash me thoroughly from my iniquity, and cleanse me from my sin… Purge me with hyssop, and I shall be clean; Wash me, and I shall be whiter than snow." (See also James 4:8; Matthew 5:8; Psalm 66:18.)

I will fill my heart with the words and thoughts of God.

Psalm 40:5
> "Many, O Lord my God, are Your wonderful works Which You have done; And Your thoughts toward us cannot be recounted to You in order; If I would declare and speak of them, they are more than can be numbered." (See also Jeremiah 29:11; Luke 1:38.)

I will fill my heart with the presence of God.

Psalm 16:11

"You will show me the path of life; In Your presence is fullness of joy; At Your right hand are pleasures forevermore." (See also Psalm 31:20; Acts 3:19.)

I will fill my mind with the things of God.

Colossians 3:1

"If then you were raised with Christ, seek those things which are above, where Christ is, sitting at the right hand of God. Set your mind on things above, not on things on the earth." (See also Ephesians 4:23; Romans 12:2; Psalm 26:2.)

I will fill my heart with meditation and reflection.

Psalm 19:14

"Let the words of my mouth and the meditation of my heart be acceptable in Your sight, O Lord, my strength and my Redeemer." (See also Psalm 49:3; 104:34.)

I will fill my heart with faith and new vision.

Galatians 2:20

"I have been crucified with Christ; it is no longer I who live, but Christ lives in me; and the life which I now live in the flesh I live by faith in the Son of God, who loved me and gave Himself for me." (See also Lamentations 3:22-25.)

I will live with a full, overflowing heart.
Ephesians 3:19

"…to know the love of Christ which passes knowledge; that you may be filled with all the fullness of God."

(See also Acts 17:28; 2 Chronicles 7:1; Psalm 126:2; John 2:7; Deuteronomy 33:23; Acts 6:3; Philippians 4:18.)

Faith Declaration #4:
I Will Have an Overflowing Heart

I will fill my heart with God's Word, prayer and praise. For out of my heart overflow the inner voice of God is heard clearly, powerfully and distinctly.

I Will Turn to God at All Times

I will turn my eyes toward God who is always ready and willing to help me in any and all of my life situations, even when I don't believe, see or feel God.

Psalm 27:9-10
"Do not hide Your face from me; Do not turn Your servant away in anger; You have been my help; Do not leave me nor forsake me, O God of my salvation. When my father and my mother forsake me, then the Lord will take care of me."

Chapter 7

I Will Turn to God at All Times

*I*t's easy to turn to God when things are going well. You just got a raise. You've met the man of your dreams. They've struck oil in your backyard and life is going great. But what happens when things begin to unravel? What happens when life begins to fall apart and suddenly God is silent. Your prayer times were powerful and you were seeing prayers answered, but now your child has cancer and God is silent. You begin to wonder if God is paying any attention at all. Does He realize what is going on in your life? Is He aware of the attacks of the enemy?

These are the times you cry out with David, "Do not hide Your face from me; Do not turn your servant away in anger; You have been my help; Do not leave me nor forsake me, O God of my salvation. When my father and my mother forsake me, then the Lord will take care of me" (Psalm 27:9-10). *The Message Bible* says, "Don't hide from me now! You've always been right there for me; don't turn your back on me now. Don't throw me out, don't abandon me; you've always kept the door open. My father and mother walked out and left me, but God took me in."

Your life has just been devastated. What do you do now? Where do you turn? The famous hymn says, "When peace like a river attendeth my way, when sorrows like sea billows roll. Whatever my lot, Thou hast taught me to say, 'It is well, it is well with my soul.'" That's easy to say when things are going well, but the hymn was written at the very place where a man had lost his four daughters in an accident. Blow one: his son died. Blow two: the Great Chicago Fire destroyed his business. Blow three: the boat his wife and four daughters were on sank and his daughters drowned. He went from being a successful and well-off businessman with a happy family to being devastated. He had lost everything. One blow, perhaps he could handle. Two blows, that took a lot more strength, but he could deal with it. But the third blow was overwhelming.

He stood on the site of the final blow, staring at the water that held the bodies of his four daughters. One blow, two blows, three blows. Where does he turn? It is well, it is well with my soul. "Though Satan should buffet, though trials should come, let this blest assurance control, that Christ hath regarded my helpless estate, and hath shed His own blood for my soul."

Like the hymn-writer Horatio Spafford, you may have been struck by the unexpected and undeserved blows of life. You could be buffeted, devastated, torn into pieces. Maybe you can't see God. You can't hear Him. You can't feel Him. You can still make a decision to turn to Him. Make a deliberate act of your will and declare: I will turn my eyes toward God who is always ready and willing to help me in any and all of my life situations, even when I don't believe, see or feel God.

Turn To God, Not Away From God

A turning point is a deliberate decision to change direction. It is a pivotal point in life. Make a deliberate decision and intentionally turn to God. "Trust in Him at all times, you people; Pour out your heart before Him; God is a refuge for us" (Psalm 62:8). Pour out your heart to God. He knows what is in your heart anyway, so open up and be honest before Him. Trust Him. 2 Chronicles 15:4 says, "When in their trouble they turned to the Lord God of Israel, and sought Him, He was found by them." When they turned, He was there.

Turn to God even when you don't feel Him.

"I go east, but he is not there. I go west, but I cannot find him. I do not see him in the north, for he is hidden. I look to the south, but he is concealed. But he knows where I am going. And when he tests me, I will come out as pure as gold. For I have stayed on God's paths; I have followed his ways and not turned aside" (Job 23:8-11, *New Living Translation*).

Job was in the middle of the worst trial of his life. He had lost everything: his home, his family, his children, and his wealth. The only thing he had left was his friends and he was probably wishing he could lose them too. His wife told him to turn away from God, but Job made a determined decision. "I will follow his ways. I will not turn away from Him." He couldn't see God. He didn't know where God was. At times He wondered if God was still there, but he still chose to trust God. "Even if God kills me, I'll trust Him."

Isaiah 8:17 says, "I will wait for the Lord, Who is hiding His face from the house of Jacob; and I will look for and hope in Him" (*Amplified Bible*). God is hiding and I can't see Him, but I will trust and hope in Him.

In his best-seller *The Purpose Driven Life*, Rick Warren wrote, "The deepest level of worship is praising God in spite of pain, thanking God during a trial, trusting Him when tempted, surrendering while suffering, and loving Him when He seems distant." God seems so far off, so separated from you in the agony you are going through, yet you choose to worship. You choose to trust. You choose to love Him.

Turn to God even when you have no faith in God.

"If we are faithless, He remains faithful; He cannot deny Himself" (2 Timothy 2:13).

Do you see the power of that verse? In the *Amplified Bible* it reads, "If we are faithless and do not believe and are untrue to

Him, He remains true, faithful to His Word and His righteous character, for He cannot deny Himself." He doesn't change! Even if we lose heart and don't trust Him, He is still trustworthy. His faithfulness and trustworthiness is not dependent on our emotions.

In *The Message Bible* this verse promises, "If we give up on Him, He does not give up – for there's no way He can be false to Himself." We can give up on Him, but He doesn't give up on us. Think about that before you read any further. It doesn't matter if you feel you have failed Him, if you didn't believe enough, pray enough, trust enough. That hasn't changed who He is or His love for you.

Engrave that on your heart. God will not forget you. He will not give up on you. He will not leave you. He will not turn His back on you. Make a deliberate decision now—turn to Him.

Psalm 27:13
"I would have lost heart, unless I had believed that I would see the goodness of the Lord In the land of the living."

Job 13:15
"Though He slay me, yet will I trust Him…"

Job 23:12
"I have not departed from the commandment of His lips; I have treasured the words of His mouth more than my necessary food."

A man stood outside his burning home in despair. His young son was still inside on the second floor but no one could get into the inferno on the ground floor and the fire department was still minutes away. Suddenly he heard a cry, his young son was leaning out the second-floor window, "Daddy! Help me!"

The man ran over to the window and looked up. "Jump! I'll catch you." The boy couldn't see his father clearly because of the smoke so he hesitated, "I can't see you, Daddy!" The father replied, "I can see you and that's all that matters."

God can see you, even if you can't see Him. He can hear you, even if you can't hear Him. Make the decision. Turn to Him. Trust even when you can't see. Trust when you can't understand. He is trustworthy. He won't fail you.

The Seven Cries of a Turning Heart

Don't hide from me!

"Do not hide your face from me..." (Psalm 27:9)

In your sorrow, adversity, pain and confusion, you may feel that God cannot be found, that He is elusive and hiding from you. Remember, He never changes. He is always there. Our feelings tell us one thing, but our feelings deceive us. Don't respond to God based on your emotions, but on the principles of His Word. Your feelings will change, but God does not.

We feel God is hiding when we have long seasons of affliction. In Psalm 13:1, David asks, "How long, O Lord? Will You forget me forever? How long will You hide Your face from me?" And in Psalm 44:24: "Why do You hide Your face, and forget our affliction and our oppression?"

It has been so long that you feel surely God has forgotten about you. If He had remembered you, He would not leave you in this situation. Since the affliction is still there, you feel God must have gotten busy and forgot about you.

We feel God is hiding when we encounter many troubles. If it was one problem, you could handle it on your own and go on with life. But there's a hornet's nest of problems that have come up and you are panicking. If God were here, wouldn't He stop this? Wouldn't He fix these problems? You need an answer and you need it now.

Psalm 69:17 says, "And do not hide Your face from Your servant, For I am in trouble; Hear me speedily." And again in Psalm 102:2: "Do not hide Your face from me in the day of my trouble; Incline Your ear to me; In the day that I call, answer me speedily." I need a speedy answer, God!

We feel God is hiding when we have unconfessed sins. "Your iniquities have separated you from your God; And your sins have hidden His face from you, so that He will not hear" (Isaiah 59:2).

Sin separates us from God, but God is quick to respond when a heart is repentant before Him. Isaiah 55:7 promises mercy, "Let the wicked forsake his way, and the unrighteous man his thoughts; let him return to the Lord, and He will have mercy on him; and to our God, for He will abundantly pardon."

There is abundant mercy and pardon in God. Turn to Him and He will turn to you. Turn to Him and repent and He will pour His mercy and grace upon your life.

Don't turn your back on me.

"…Do not turn…" (Psalm 27:9)

2 Chronicles 30:9 promises, "For if you return to the Lord, your brethren and your children will be treated with compassion by those who lead them captive, so that they may come back to this land; for the Lord your God is gracious and merciful, and will not turn His face from you if you return to Him." If you turn to God, He will not turn away from you.

The prodigal son's father had every reason to refuse his son and turn his back on him. His son had betrayed him and had ruined his life. When the son came to the door and asked to see his father, the father could have sent a servant out to deal with him. The servant could have either told the son to leave or sent him away from the father's house to the servant's quarters to earn his food. The father would have been justified to do that.

Instead, it says the father saw the son coming. How many days had he stood and looked down that empty road and wondered where his son was? But today was different. Today there was a beggar in ragged clothes stumbling down the road. And the father recognized him.

The son probably wouldn't have recognized himself, but the father recognized him. Even from afar off there was something in the father's heart that said, "That's my son!" And the father ran. He couldn't wait. He ran. He ran toward the son and grabbed him in his arms and hugged the filthy, unwashed mess that his son had become.

The son limped toward the father. The father ran toward the son. When you turn toward God, He doesn't turn away in disgust or disdain. He runs toward you. You may turn hesitantly, brokenly, stumbling over your feet as you move toward Him, but He is running toward you, arms wide open. Take your eyes off the ground and look up. You'll see Him coming.

Don't be angry with me.

"...Do not turn your servant away in anger..." (Psalm 27:9)

Don't be angry when my prayer request is pushing the envelope. God had already granted five requests. Each time Abraham asked for a little bit more. "If there are 50 righteous? 45? 40? 30?" How far would Abraham go? How far would God's patience stretch? But God didn't get angry with Abraham; He granted each request (Genesis 18:30-32).

Don't be angry when I go over the line to ask for something. Gideon had already asked God for a sign twice and both times God had honored his request. How many signs does it take for someone to believe God? Gideon had to ask one more time, one more sign, and God answered (Judges 6:39).

Don't be angry when my heart is turned away from God's purposes. God did become angry with Solomon "because his heart had turned from the Lord God of Israel, who had appeared to him twice" (1 Kings 11:9). God had come to Solomon twice and now Solomon was chasing after his own desires.

But Jeremiah reminds us that even though God does get angry, he does not stay angry forever. He is a God of mercy and calls the backslidden to return to Him. "'Return, backsliding Israel,' says the Lord; 'I will not cause My anger to fall on you. For I am merciful,' says the Lord; 'I will not remain angry forever'"(Jeremiah 3:12). Isaiah 12:1 also promises God's mercy: "And in that day you will say: 'O Lord, I will praise You; Though You were angry with me, Your anger is turned away, and You comfort me.'" (See also Psalm 69:16.)

Even when God is angry, He is a God of mercy. If you turn back to Him, He will turn to you. He will not reject a repentant heart.

Don't stop helping me.

"…You have been my help…" (Psalm 27:9)

Help me, God, even when I don't deserve your help. Even if I got myself into this mess, please help me. Help me when I have exhausted my resources. When I'm at the end of my rope and don't know which way to turn, help me. When I have no strength to stand and no wisdom to know how to handle my situation, help me.

Help me when I have lost hope. Help me when I've given up. Put new hope into my spirit. Put new strength into my arms. Help me when I have been fighting for a long time and there seems to be no end in sight. Don't stop helping me.

Hebrews 4:16

"Let us therefore come boldly to the throne of grace, that we may obtain mercy and find grace to help in time of need."

2 Chronicles 32:8

"'With him is an arm of flesh; but with us is the Lord our God, to help us and to fight our battles.' And the people were strengthened by the words of Hezekiah king of Judah."

Psalm 22:19

"You, O Lord, do not be far from Me; O My Strength, hasten to help Me!"

Psalm 33:20

"Our soul waits for the Lord; He is our help and our shield."

Psalm 44:26

"Arise for our help, and redeem us for Your mercies' sake."

Isaiah 41:10,13

"Fear not, for I am with you; Be not dismayed, for I am your God. I will strengthen you, yes, I will help you, I will uphold you with My righteous right hand... For I, the Lord your God, will hold your right hand, saying to you, 'Fear not, I will help you.'"

(See also Genesis 49:25; Exodus 18:4; Deuteronomy 33:29; Psalm 46:5.)

Don't reject me.

"...Do not leave me..." (Psalm 27:9)

Rejection is such a great part of our society. Parents have rejected children, children have rejected parents and friends have rejected friends, but God doesn't reject us. The English word reject comes from a Latin word meaning "to throw back." Reject is what you do when you are fishing: throw it back; it's too small. Throw it back; it's not the right kind.

When someone has been rejected, they become negative. They lose the spirit of expectation for anything good to happen. Negativity is a stronghold in the mind that Satan takes advantage of and uses to cause depression, fear, and doubt.

Guilt and shame breed feelings of rejection. They give voice to the cry, "Do not cast me away from Your presence, and do not take Your Holy Spirit from me" (Psalm 51:11).

Rejection is not something God does to us. He never throws us back as inferior in quality. He doesn't throw us back because we aren't good enough. In Genesis 28:15 God promises, "Behold, I am with you and will keep you wherever you go, and will bring you back to this land; for I will not leave you until I have done what I have spoken to you." He promises He won't walk out and leave. Jesus repeats this in the New Testament in John 14:18. "I will not leave you orphans. I will come to you." God doesn't reject anyone.

Don't abandon me.

"...nor forsake me..."(Psalm 27:9)

Don't give up on me. Don't leave me. Abandon has the idea of giving something up with no intention of ever returning to reclaim it. Abandonment gives someone up as a lost cause.

Here is God's response to those who fear He will abandon them:

Deuteronomy 31:6

"Be strong and of good courage, do not fear nor be afraid of them; for the Lord your God, He is the One who goes with you. He will not leave you nor forsake you."

Psalm 37:28

"For the Lord loves justice, and does not forsake His saints; They are preserved forever, But the descendants of the wicked shall be cut off."

Hebrews 13:5

"For He Himself has said, 'I will never leave you nor forsake you.'"

Don't close the door on me.

"...The Lord will take care of me..." (Psalm 27:9)

When a friend closes the door on a relationship, it's over. It's finished. When a parent closes the door on a child, they are shutting that child out of their life. God never closes the door on you. He will not shut you out of relationship with Him.

In Hosea 2:15, God is talking about Israel when He says, "I will give her her vineyards from there, and the Valley of Achor as a door of hope; She shall sing there, as in the days of her youth, as in the day when she came up from the land of Egypt."

God had every right to close the door on Israel. He had given her chance after chance. For hundreds of years He had disciplined, He had mercy, He judged, He gave grace. Yet Israel simply refused to follow Him. She continually turned away from Him and turned to sin.

The Valley of Achor was a place of judgment. It was a place where an entire family was stoned because of their sin. Yet this was the place God was opening up as a door of hope. Even though you have sinned, even though you have been judged, there is still an open door of hope. There is still an open door of mercy. All you have to do is walk through it. The door is open. It's up to you.

Turning to God By Waiting on Him

What do you do when God is silent? Your world has fallen apart. Unexplainable events have laid your world in ruins. You are confused and hurting and God is silent. You cry out to Him, "Don't reject me! Don't close the door on me! Don't stop helping me!" And He is silent. David knew that feeling. He despaired in Psalm 28:1-2, "To You I will cry, O Lord my Rock: do not be silent to me, lest, if You are silent to me, I become like those who go down to the pit. Hear the voice of my supplications when I cry to You, when I lift up my hands toward Your holy sanctuary."

Job felt this when he lamented in Job 23:8-9, "Look, I go forward, but He is not there, and backward, but I cannot perceive Him; when He works on the left hand, I cannot behold Him; when He turns to the right hand, I cannot see Him." God may be working, but I see no evidence that He is even around. How do you live in those situations?

Wait on God passionately.

"I sought the Lord, and He heard me, and delivered me from all my fears" (Psalm 34:4).

Passionate is the opposite of indifferent or passive. Passionate waiting is active and alert. What is the difference between passive waiting and active waiting, between apathetic waiting and passionate waiting? Listening obedience. Waiting requires listening for the voice of God and responding instantly to that voice.

"But I can't hear God!" Even when you do not hear the personal voice of God speaking directly into your situation, you have the written word of God that is unchanging. When you cannot hear God, return to what He has written and line your life up with that. As you remain in His word, remain on your knees and remain actively listening, you will find yourself positioned for His voice when He speaks.

Wait on God patiently.

"I waited patiently for the Lord; and He inclined unto me, and heard my cry" (Psalm 40:1).

Waiting on God patiently is holding out and waiting for God's time and will. To be patient is to plant your feet and stand firm when under pressure. It is to plant your feet firm in God and refuse to be moved. The earth may shake, the mountains may move, but the stability in your spirit is the quiet confidence that your God is unchanging. He is still God. He is still with you. He still cares and He is still able. It doesn't matter how you feel. Your feelings do not change who He is.

When a wild doe senses danger, she will hide her baby in a safe place and then act as a decoy for the animal that is threatening the safety of her fawn. Even at that young age, the fawn understands the principle of waiting patiently. He will remain where his mother left him even though he cannot sense her anywhere. The appearance is that she has deserted him, but he patiently waits. She can lead the mountain lion or bear on a chase through the woods and be gone for hours. The fawn waits. He waits patiently for his mother to return because he trusts her. Learn to wait quietly and patiently. No matter how things appear, God has not forsaken you.

Patience fixes its eyes on Christ. Hebrews 12:2 says, "Looking unto Jesus, the author and finisher of our faith, who for the joy that was set before Him endured the cross, despising the shame, and has sat down at the right hand of the throne of God." The *Amplified Bible* says, "Look away from all that will distract." Don't look at your circumstances. Look at Christ. Focus on Him. Trust Him. Be dependent on Him. You can't make things happen. You can't force circumstances to change; only He can do that. So wait patiently. Wait for His timing.

Wait on God purposefully.

"As the deer pants for the water brooks, so pants my soul for You, O God" (Psalm 42:1).

In the Greek, the word wait has the intensity of leaning forward, with your gaze fixed on what you are expecting to receive, reaching out to grasp it. A toddler sitting in his high chair "waits" for his mother to feed him: mouth wide open, hands reaching and grasping, feet kicking. This is a word of intensity, not passivity. Your eyes are fixed in eager anticipation, stretching toward Him.

Martin Luther once watched his dog sitting beside the table watching him eat. The dog's ears were alert and every fiber in the dog's body was taut and poised, waiting for Luther to drop a scrap of food. As he looked in amusement, Luther commented, "Oh, if I could only pray the way this dog watches the meat! All his thoughts are concentrated on the piece of meat. Otherwise he has no thought, wish or hope."[1]

Wait on God prayerfully.

"Therefore if there is any consolation in Christ, if any comfort of love, if any fellowship of the Spirit, if any affection and mercy, fulfill my joy by being like-minded, having the same love, being of one accord, of one mind" (Philippians 2:1-2).

Do not neglect your spiritual man. An undeveloped spirit will hinder your ability to hear God, to wait on God, and to follow God. Practice the spiritual disciplines of the Word of God, prayer, worship, and fellowship with other Christians.

Pray prayers of thanksgiving, giving appreciation and gratefulness to God. If you can't think of anything to be thankful for, find something. Colossians 4:2 commands, "Continue earnestly in prayer, being vigilant in it with thanksgiving."

Pray prayers of praise, exalting God and worshipping Him. Pray prayers about the greatness of God. Go to the Psalms and begin to pray some of David's prayers, prayers that remind you of who your God is.

Pray prayers of intercession and petition. Pray for others, not just for yourself. Intercede for others.

Pray prayers of dedication, yielding your life to God. Follow the example of Judah in 2 Chronicles 15:12. "They entered into a covenant to seek the Lord God of their fathers with all their heart and with all their soul." F.B. Meyer said, "Give your mind, your will, your power of choice to God. Make Him first. Ask Him to take the helm of your life, and to control, inspire and direct its every movement. Crown Him King."[2]

Pray prayers of confession, asking for forgiveness. Allow no hidden sin to take root in your life. Confess your sins with the confidence that "If we confess our sins, He is faithful and just to forgive us our sins and to cleanse us from all unrighteousness" (1 John 1:9).

Pray prayers of communion and intimacy with God. His heart is toward you. He desires a personal relationship with you. He does not hold you at arm's length, but He brings you near and embraces you to His heart. Respond to Him.

Throughout scripture we find repeated references to God seeking out those who would respond to Him and have an intimate friendship with Him. In the Garden of Eden, He walked with Adam and Eve and conversed with them. He called Abraham his friend and shared with him his plans for the city of Sodom. He called the nation of Israel to come to the mountain of the Lord so that He could speak to them, but they were terrified and would not. God instead spoke with Moses "face to face as a man would speak with a friend."

This isn't just Old Testament. In John 15:14-16 Jesus makes and amazing disclosure that we often don't fully treasure. "No longer do I call you servants, for a servant does not know what his master is doing; but I have called you friends, for all things that I heard from My Father I have made known to you." He said, "You are my friends. Let's talk." The Almighty Creator desires to talk with you, His friend.

Wait on God with a listening ear.

"My sheep hear My voice, and I know them, and they follow Me" (John 10:27).

Don't be so busy talking to God that you forget to listen. In your prayer times, plan for times of stillness to listen to the voice of God. John 15 says that Jesus wants to tell you things, but you have to be listening in order to hear them. Your eternal destiny is determined by how you respond to the voice and leading of God.

Wait on God persistently.

"Lead me in thy truth, and teach me: for thou art the God of my salvation; on thee do I wait all the day" (Psalm 25:5).

"But if we hope for what we do not see, we eagerly wait for it with perseverance" (Romans 8:25).

Don't give up. If the answer doesn't come right away, keep waiting. Persistence requires trusting God, knowing He will act when He is ready and trusting Him in the meantime.

Wait on God expectantly.

"And you will seek Me and find Me, when you search for Me with all your heart" (Jeremiah 29:13).

Expect God to speak. Expect Him to answer. Wait with anticipation. Wait with a confidence and assurance that God will reveal himself and that He will accomplish His word.

Be ready. Be prepared to receive. A good beggar always has his hand out. He doesn't sit with his hands in his pocket as you walk by. He puts that hand right in front of your face and leaves it there until you put something in it. Have that attitude toward God. Put your hand out and leave it there, expecting Him to fill it with Himself.

Watch. Be looking. Fix your eyes on God. If you're asleep, you'll never know the opportunities you missed because your eyes were closed.

Wait joyfully. Psalm 37:4 says, "Delight yourself also in the Lord, and He shall give you the desires of your heart." Wait with a joy in seeking God. Joy sees beyond the present reality to the eternal reality. Joy is not based on your present circumstances but on the eternal truth of your God. Wait joyfully.

Psalm 43:4 tells us to praise joyfully: "Then I will go to the altar of God, to God my exceeding joy; and on the harp I will praise You, O God, my God."

Turning to God is simply setting your eyes, your hopes, your dreams, your expectations, your joy on Him. Fix your heart on Him as if your very existence depends on Him. Even when life contradicts His word and every hope and dream is dashed, set your eyes on Him and choose to believe that everything else in life is meaningless without Him.

Faith Declaration #5: I Will Turn to God at All Times

I will turn my eyes toward God who is always ready and willing to help me in any and all of my life situations, even when I don't believe, see or feel God.

I Will Walk on a Level Path

I will choose a lifestyle of integrity and I will walk according to the principles of God's word. I will learn God's ways and walk on a level path.

Psalm 27:11-12

"Teach me Your way, O Lord, and lead me in a smooth path, because of my enemies. Do not deliver me to the will of my adversaries; for false witnesses have risen against me, and such as breathe out violence."

Chapter 8

I Will Walk on a Level Path

The journey of life is spoken of as a path we take, a road we choose to go down. It is a broad way or a narrow way. Proverbs 16:17 says, "The highway of the upright is to depart from evil; He who keeps his way preserves his soul." The believer is responsible to walk on a level path, not an up and down path, but a path having no part higher than another. It is a steady path, unwavering, balanced and progressive.

Isaiah describes the highway we should choose to travel on. "A highway shall be there, and a road, and it shall be called the Highway of Holiness. The unclean shall not pass over it, but it shall be for others" (Isaiah 35:8). We have been built to go fast on God's highway, a freeway, a place to move forward rapidly without stumbling or falling. It is a level path.

The unshakable life is lived out by consistently following God's principles and God's laws in God's word. Isaiah 40:3-5 describes the unshakable person who will experience the favor and blessing of the Lord. "The voice of one crying in the wilderness: 'Prepare the way of the Lord; Make straight in the desert a highway for our God. Every valley shall be exalted and every mountain and hill brought low; The crooked places shall be made straight and the rough places smooth; The glory of the Lord shall be revealed, and all flesh shall see it together; For the mouth of the Lord has spoken.'"

Our level path is smooth. It is having a life without unnecessary bends and curves or irregularities, a straight path that wastes no time and energy. David prays in Psalms 27:11-12

"Teach me Your way, O Lord, and lead me in a smooth path, because of my enemies. Do not deliver me to the will of my adversaries; for false witnesses have risen against me, and such as breathe out violence."

The unshakable person will face the adversaries of life, the false witnesses, those who seek to destroy his life. Psalm 125:5 warns us not to be pressured into going down the crooked path. "As for such as turn aside to their crooked ways, the Lord shall lead them away with the workers of iniquity." We live as the children of God without fault in the midst of a crooked and perverse generation (Philippians 2:15). This is why our unshakable life declaration, made with faith and determination, is of utmost importance. Our faith declaration based on Psalm 27:11-12 is "I will choose a lifestyle of integrity and I will walk according to the principles of God's word. I will learn God's ways and walk on a level path."

A Level Path

A level path is one that is direct and level. It is a path that is free from obstacles. There's nothing there to stumble over. If we are going to walk in a level path, we must have an upright life. An upright life is one that is lived in accordance with the righteousness of God. If you live a life of sin, you will have a life full of stumbling blocks and obstacles, but a life of righteousness will be a life lived with a level and clear path to walk. (See also Proverbs 2:15; 8:8; Isaiah 45:2; 62:10.)

The Way You Live Determines Your Path

The way you live your life is reflected by your moral character, actions and behavior. Your way is the life you are living, your lifestyle. It is the moral choices that you make today and the character that is being built into your life by those choices.

Your way does not form overnight. It is not a one-decision choice. It is formed by a series of decisions, a pattern of behavior and a habit of ongoing actions. (See 2 Chronicles 6:27; 11:17; 20:32; Job 23:10; Psalm 1:6; 27:11.)

The Path You Take Leads to Your Destiny

The path you take is your life journey, the direction that your lifestyle takes you. Proverbs 14:12 tells us, "There is a way that seems right to a man, but its end is the way of death." You choose your lifestyle, but that lifestyle will lead you either to death or to life. The way that you choose determines your path. The choices you make determine your lifestyle and your lifestyle can determine your destiny.

The Eastern Continental Divide runs through Oak Park, a Chicago suburb. If raindrops fall on the west side of that divide, they flow down the Mississippi to the warm Gulf of Mexico. If they fall on the east side, they flow through the Great Lakes, over Niagara Falls and end in the cold North Atlantic. The path of those raindrops is decided by a mere few inches. Two raindrops can be falling side by side, yet if one falls on the west side of a building located on the divide it ends up thousands of miles away from the raindrop that falls on the east side. Just a few inches, just a puff of breeze, that is all that separates the ultimate destinies of these two raindrops. The path you are taking can be changed by simple decisions that affect your destiny.

What kind of destiny do you want? What kind of person do you want to be in 30 years? The decisions you make now will determine your future and your destiny. I made a simple decision when I was a teenager. A friend of mine who had been drinking asked me to come with him. I made a choice. That was not going to be my lifestyle. That simple decision led to a path that has profoundly impacted my destiny because my friend was killed that night. If I had made a different decision, my destiny would have been to die beside him.

Several years later I made another decision that changed my path and my destiny. I decided to go to college. My path turned me away from one destiny toward a different destiny that included moving to Portland where I met my wife and formed life-long relationships that affected my ministry and connected me to the church I would pastor.

Proverbs 4:18-19 tells us, "The path of the just is like the shining sun, that shines ever brighter unto the perfect day. The way of the wicked is like darkness; they do not know what makes them stumble." (See also Proverbs 3:5-6; 11:5; 2:15; 3:23.)

The Path You Choose Can Destroy Your Destiny

"The paths of their way turn aside, they go nowhere and perish" (Job 6:18).

The path of sinful behavior

Psalm 1:1 praises those who turn away from sin: "Blessed is the man who walks not in the counsel of the ungodly, nor stands in the path of sinners, nor sits in the seat of the scornful."

Sin means to miss the mark. Sin aims at righteousness and finds only self-righteousness. It aims at doing good and hits self-enthronement. Sin goes beyond the line and wanders from the path. It falls when it should stand. Sin neglects to hear and refuses to obey. Sin is self-will, self-exaltation, self-enthronement, self-centeredness, self-sufficiency and self-ascendancy.

Proverbs 1:15 warns, "My son, do not walk in the way with them; keep your foot from their path."

The path of immorality

1 Corinthians 6:18 commands, "Flee sexual immorality." This isn't a suggestion or just a good idea. It's a command. Paul says run as far and as fast as you can from immorality. Don't stand around thinking about it, but the minute it comes up get out of there. That's what Joseph did. When Potiphar's wife tried to seduce him, he ran so quick he left his coat behind. He didn't go back to get it. He didn't worry about losing it. He ran.

Why is this so important? Read the rest of 1 Corinthians 6:18-19: "Every sin that a man does is outside the body, but he who commits sexual immorality sins against his own body. Or do you not know that your body is the temple of the Holy Spirit who is in you, whom you have from God, and you are not your own?"

Immorality is a sin that destroys your soul. It doesn't just have external affects, but it affects you internally. Sexual encounters involve the spirit, mind and emotions of a person and immorality has a profound impact on them.

Bring your sexuality before God and lay in on the altar. If you have sinned in the past, now is the time to stop. If you are trying to see how close you can get to the line before you go over, stop. Flee.

1 Thessalonians 4:3-7 states, "For this is the will of God, your sanctification: that you should abstain from sexual immorality; that each of you should know how to possess his own vessel in sanctification and honor, not in passion of lust, like the Gentiles who do not know God; that no one should take advantage of and defraud his brother in this matter, because the Lord is the avenger of all such, as we also forewarned you and

testified. For God did not call us to uncleanness, but in holiness."

The path of forgetting God

Psalm 106:21 says, "They forgot God their Savior, who had done great things in Egypt." They had seen the hand of God work miracles. They had walked on dry ground through a parted sea. They had seen God turn water into blood, bring plagues, heal diseases, and feed them with food that miraculously appeared on the ground every morning. They had seen the great things God had done, but they forgot Him. To forget is to get so busy and preoccupied that you lay something down and lose it. It is lost through lack of attention, lack of valuing.

What have you mislaid? Your Bible? Your prayer life? Your attitudes? Your commitment to God? What are the things you have allowed to preoccupy you? Your family, caring for your children, attending church, spending time with friends, working, volunteering, exercising, recreation time? These aren't wrong things. They are good things, yet if you allow them to push God into the background, you will find yourself forgetting God.

Make God your priority. Make spending time with Him something highly valued and greatly desired. One morning at a time, begin to create a habit of spending time with Him.

In one region of Africa, the believers each had their own special place outside the village where they went to pray in solitude. The villagers reached these "prayer rooms" by using their own private footpaths through the brush. When grass began to grow over one of these trails, it was evident that the person to whom it belonged was not praying very much. Whenever anyone noticed an overgrown "Prayer path," he or she would go to the person and lovingly warn, "Friend, there's grass on your path!"

Friend, is there grass on your path? Have you begun to neglect that time with God? Have you set your Bible aside in favor of the urgent things that clamor for your attention? Start trampling that grass down again. Make your relationship with God the top priority in your life. Value His presence more than you value anything else, for without His presence nothing else matters.

The path of darkness

The path of darkness is the path of misery, destruction, death, ignorance, sorrow. It literally is the opposite of light. It is the path that is in opposition to everything about God. Proverbs 2:13 says, "From those who leave the paths of uprightness to walk in the ways of darkness." Don't allow anything in your life that is in opposition to God.

1 John 1:5-7 tells us that "God is light and in Him is no darkness at all. If we say that we have fellowship with Him, and walk in darkness, we lie and do not practice the truth. But if we walk in the light as He is in the light, we have fellowship with one another, and the blood of Jesus Christ His Son cleanses us from all sin."

Lot Chose a Path to Success That Destroyed His Destiny

Lot had been raised under the tutelage of Abraham, a man who walked in the ways of God. He had seen the fruit in Abraham's life as a result of Abraham's choice to walk the level path. Yet when Lot was faced with his own decision, instead of praying, "Teach me Your way, O Lord", he "lifted his eyes and saw" and made a decision based on what was the most appealing.

Lot chose based on the natural, not the spiritual.

Genesis 13:10 says, "And Lot lifted his eyes and saw all the plain of the Jordan, that it was well watered everywhere (before the Lord destroyed Sodom and Gomorrah) like the garden of the Lord, like the land of Egypt as you go toward Zoar."

Lot looked with his natural eyes and saw what was appealing to him. It was beautiful. It looked like a wonderful decision. If you had a choice between living in Hawaii or in the Sahara Desert, which would you chose? But Lot only saw with his natural eye. He didn't look with the eyes of his spirit to see that choices that appear outwardly appealing can be detrimental to his spiritual destiny.

Lot chose for himself by himself.

Genesis 13:11 says that Lot "chose for Himself all the plain of Jordan." He insisted on his rights. His decision was based on selfishness. He didn't ask what God wanted, but He chose based on his own selfish desires.

Lot chose separation from the godly influences in his life.

Lot separated himself from Abraham. He went one way and left Abraham to go another. It is dangerous for a person to cut himself off from religious privileges for the sake of material gain alone. It is dangerous to isolate yourself from godly influence and surround yourself only with those who do not live according to the same biblical principles that you do.

Lot chose temporary success that led to a failed destiny.

When the angels came to Sodom, Genesis 19:1 says they found Lot "sitting in the gate of Sodom." To sit at the gates of the city was to sit in a place of honor. Those who sat there were men of power and authority, men who were respected and honored. Lot found success in Sodom. Isn't that a sign that

God was blessing his decision? Bad decisions sometimes lead to temporary success, but the ultimate end is a failed destiny. In the end Lot lost his wealth, his honor, his family and his respect. In the end, even his daughters did not respect him. A wrong decision in order to gain temporary success yields painful results.

The Result of Wrong Ways That Lead to Wrong Paths

Oscar Wilde is a famous poet and playwright from the 19th century. Toward the end of his life he said, "The gods had given me almost everything. But I let myself be lured into long spells of senseless and sensual ease...Tired of being on the heights, I deliberately went to the depths in search for new sensation. What the paradox was to me in the sphere of thought, perversity became to me in the sphere of passion. I grew careless of the lives of others. I took pleasure where it pleased me, and passed on. I forgot that every little action of the common day makes or unmakes character, and that therefore what one has done in the secret chamber, one has some day to cry aloud from the house-top. I ceased to be lord over myself. I was no longer the captain of my soul, and did not know it. I allowed pleasure to dominate me. I ended in horrible disgrace."[1]

The Path You Choose Can Fulfill Your Destiny

The path of the Lord

The path of the Lord is a sure path, one that we can walk without stumbling. Psalm 17:5 says, "Uphold my steps in Your paths, that my footsteps may not slip." The path of the Lord is a path of mercy and truth, according to Psalm 25:10: "All the paths of the Lord are mercy and truth, to such as keep His covenant and His testimonies." (See also Proverbs 4:11; 25:4; 3:6; Isaiah 2:3.)

The path of God's presence

"You will show me the path of life; In Your presence is fullness of joy; At Your right hand are pleasures forevermore" (Psalms 16:11).

In *A Closer Walk*, Brother Lawrence observed, "To practice the presence of God is to live in the conscious awareness of Our Father, engaging in quiet, joyful, and continuous conversation with Him. It means we live an inner life of unceasing prayer and we strive for all we think, say, and do to be a reflection of what is pleasing to God."[2]

The presence path is a path of worship and prayerful intercession for the maturing believer. The presence of God is not merely some force or influence that we seek, but a personal, real, life-changing presence of a living God who abides in us and dwells among us. We must nurture a passion for the presence of God.

The straight path

Hebrews 12:13 states, "and make straight paths for your feet, so that what is lame may not be dislocated, but rather be healed."

A straight path is a path of integrity and principle. It's a path of good decisions. Live a principled life, a life of righteousness.

In Psalm 23:3, David says of the Lord: "He restores my soul; He leads me in the paths of righteousness for His name's sake. "

There is harmony and inner peace to be found in following a moral compass that points in the same direction regardless of fashions or trends. A path of integrity is not hindered by bad circumstances or life surprises. Integrity leads straight and persistent. Proverbs 2:20 says, "So you may walk in the way of goodness, and keep to the paths of righteousness."

The path of God's commandments

Walk according to the Word of God. Psalms 119:35 says, "Make me walk in the path of Your commandments, for I delight in it." Let His Word be your guide in decision-making (Psalm 119:105). The Bible is called the Word of God because it is God speaking to man. It is communication and revelation from God to man, showing him in a clear, concise, intelligible and rational way his interest, duty, privileges and the reasonable service that God requires of him.

The Word of God is to be read, respected, memorized and hidden in the heart and obeyed in every part of life. The word is described in Psalm 119 as the law, which guides, directs and instructs you in the way of righteousness, making your path straight.

The Word of God is a statute. It marks out your way, describing the line of conduct you are to pursue and demonstrating the values you are to observe. Psalm 119 also refers to precepts which take notice of the way your life is going and speaks to the concerns and duties of life. As commandments, the Word of God shows you what you should do and what you should not do. It commands obedience.

The testimony of the Word of God points ahead to the good things that are to come, bearing witness to the hope of the future. Psalm 119 also describes the Word as judgments that appraise your words and works, provide the rules by which life should be regulated, and help you to discern what is right and wrong.

The Word of God is the truth. It is the law that is established, steady, confirmed and ordered in all things, which should be believed on the authority of God. It is to be trusted as an infallible testimony from Him who cannot lie or deceive.

The Word of God is the way. It is the way in which man must walk in order to be safe, holy and happy. The Word of God is righteousness. It teaches a man to give everyone their due (God, man, himself) for every man has duties to God, his neighbor and himself. This word is applied to God's judgments, testimonies and commandments. They are all righteous, give to all their due and require what is due from every one.

Abraham Chose a Path of Service That Fulfilled His Destiny

Abraham chose to walk in integrity and humility before god, seeking God's will over his own will. It was a choice that God honored and led him in a smooth path, providing protection from and victory over his enemies.

Abraham chose based on the spiritual, not the natural.

"And he went on his journey from the South as far as Bethel, to the place where his tent had been at the beginning, between Bethel and Ai, to the place of the altar which he had made there at first. And there Abram called on the name of the Lord" (Genesis 13:2-4).

Abraham could have chosen any place to live, but he went to the place of the altar. He went to the place of the presence of God. There were unlimited possibilities in front of him, but he chose based on the presence of God.

Abraham chose for the good of others.

Abraham chose self-denial and self-sacrifice rather than self-promotion and self-fulfillment. Genesis 13:8 records this exchange: "So Abram said to Lot, 'Please let there be no strife between you and me, and between my herdsmen and your herdsmen; for we are brethren. Is not the whole land before you? Please separate from me. If you take the left, then I will go to the right; or, if you go to the right, then I will go to the left.'"

This doesn't agree with world philosophy! Abraham was the elder statesman, the one who had sacrificed to build a good home for his family, including Lot. Lot was the younger, his nephew. He was young and ambitious. Let him take the hard path and let the older man who had already worked hard all his life take the easier path.

That wasn't Abraham's choice. He displayed godly character in his interaction with Lot. He was unselfish, seeking Lot's well-being over his own. He was generous and gave Lot the choice of the country. He valued his relationship with Lot more than his ability to gain wealth and power.

Abraham did not insist on his rights but was willing to serve the younger man, giving up what seemed to be the best. He trusted that God would do better for him than he could do for himself. Abraham lived according to the Proverbs 3:5-6 principle. "Trust in the Lord with all your heart, and lean not on your own understanding; In all your ways acknowledge Him, and He shall direct your paths."

Abraham chose self-control.

Abraham kept his eye fastened on God. Lot lifted his eyes and looked at the country. He looked in the natural and coveted the good things he saw. Abraham looked at God and only God. He could have demanded his rights of seniority and family headship. He could have divided the land into equal sections of good and bad and allowed Lot to choose half, thus maintaining some control over the decision. Instead Abraham controlled his own desires and allowed Lot full choice of everything he saw.

Abraham chose an eternal destiny over the appearance of success.

Abraham gave up the successful choice. He gave up the superior land and chose the inferior because he saw something that Lot did not. He saw that his life was in the hands of God and God would open and close doors. His focus was on God, not his personal success. He trusted that the God who promised him the land in chapter 12 was the God who would see that accomplished. He didn't depend on his own strength and ability to make it happen; he trusted God.

God honored Abraham's choice and said in Genesis 13:14-17, "Lift your eyes now and look from the place where you are — northward, southward, eastward, and westward; for all the land which you see I give to you and your descendants forever. And I will make your descendants as the dust of the earth; so that if a man could number the dust of the earth, then your descendants also could be numbered. Arise, walk in the land through its length and its width, for I give it to you." All the land was his.

Choosing a Path of Unshakable Destiny

Align your life under the Word of God.

Your standards and convictions must be shaped by the Word of God. Whatever the issue – friendships marriage, love, money, morality – the word of God is the final authority for your life.

You must know the Word of God. Study it, read it, memorize it. Know what it says about situations in life. When you have a life decision, go to the word and begin to look to see what the Bible says about that issue. The Bible is applicable to your life today. It is not an outdated book that does not fit in our culture. It is a divinely inspired word from God that encompasses all cultures.

It isn't enough merely to know what the Bible says; you must apply it. You must live in obedience to what God says through His written word. Never allow yourself to be swayed to go against the principles of the Word of God.

Hebrews 4:12
"For the word of God is living and powerful, and sharper than any two-edged sword, piercing even to the division of soul and spirit, and of joints and marrow, and is a discerner of the thoughts and intents of the heart."

2 Timothy 3:16
"All Scripture is given by inspiration of God, and is profitable for doctrine, for reproof, for correction, for instruction in righteousness."

Colossians 2:8
"Beware lest anyone cheat you through philosophy and empty deceit, according to the tradition of men, according to the basic principles of the world, and not according to Christ."

Matthew 4:4
"But He answered and said, 'It is written, "Man shall not live by bread alone, but by every word that proceeds from the mouth of God."'"

Seek counsel and gain wisdom from others.
Have a teachable spirit. Be ready to receive instruction and responsible to react promptly and obediently to what you learn. Psalm 25:4 says, "Show me Your ways, O Lord; teach

me Your paths." (See also Psalm 25:12; 32:8; 86:11; 119:26; 119:66.)

Learn from the lifestyles and decision making processes of wise men and women of God. Observe the way they live, watch the paths they take and learn from them. Allow their life to keep you from making mistakes. But don't just learn from their successes, learn from their failures. Learn from other people's mistakes. If people are making unwise decisions and ruining their lives, watch what they are doing and don't do it! Proverbs 13:20 says, "He who walks with wise men will be wise, but the companion of fools will be destroyed." Hang around wise people. Study them. Become their friends. Learn from them.

Learn from your own mistakes. If you don't learn from your mistakes, they will swallow up your destiny. Two teachers applied for the same vice-principal position at a high school. One had been teaching for eight years and the other one for twenty. Everyone expected the teacher with more years of experience to get the job, but the other person was chosen. When the disgruntled applicant questioned the board, they said, "She has eight years of experience and you have one year of experience repeated twenty times."

Don't repeat your same mistakes over and over again. Learn from an experience and do things differently the next time. The English word learn comes from an old German word meaning "to find or follow a track." You don't learn if you only find the track, you must follow it. Learning isn't just gaining knowledge. It is using that knowledge, living by it. As an old farmer said, "You don't learn anything the second time you're kicked by a mule."

Listen to the voice of the Holy Spirit.

"I will instruct you and teach you in the way you should go; I will guide you with My eye" (Psalm 32:8). Listen to the voice of the Spirit speak to you through the Bible, through the counsel of others and through the still small voice in your inner man that say, "This is the way. Walk in it."

Spend time in prayer, talking to God and listening. Make it a priority in your life. Don't start a day until you have set time aside to listen to His voice. Don't make a decision until you have talked it to Him about it. Jesus said, "My sheep hear My voice, and I know them, and they follow Me" (John 10:27). Listen to His voice until you recognize it in the dark as well as in the light.

In his book "The Secret of Guidance," F.B. Meyer said, "It is not necessary to make long prayer, but it is essential to be much alone with God; waiting at His door; hearkening for His voice: lingering in the garden of Scripture for the coming of the Lord God in the dawn or cool of the day. No number of meetings, no fellowship with Christian friends, no amount of Christian activity can compensate for the neglect of the still hour."[3]

Keys to Choosing the Right Path

When making a decision, ask yourself these questions:

1. What does the Bible clearly say?
2. Have I used the common sense God gave me?
3. Have I sought mature counsel?
4. Is this in agreement with the desires that God has placed in my heart?

People Who Chose Paths of Destiny

Daniel: Chose not to compromise principles.

"But Daniel purposed in his heart that he would not defile himself with the portion of the king's delicacies, nor with the wine which he drank; therefore he requested of the chief of the eunuchs that he might not defile himself" (Daniel 1:8).

Daniel was being held captive in a foreign land. No one would have known if he had compromised his principles. If they had known, they probably would have excused him due to the extenuating circumstances. But Daniel knew and he knew God knew. He had purposed in his heart that he would live according to the principles of God's word. He had made a decision and that decision pointed his life in a certain direction. That direction led to a great destiny.

It was a simple decision. It only related to food. He would not eat it. That little decision opened doors for him. Others saw that he was a person of integrity and he began to advance quickly in the political ranks of the Babylonian society.

The next decision was a lot bigger. If he prayed, he would be killed. He could have changed his habits and hid his principles, but he would not compromise. He would not change his direction in life because he was headed towards a destiny of life in God. That decision moved him, not just closer to his destiny in God, but to a destiny of leadership in the ranks of the Babylonian court. He chose not to compromise and that decision forever altered his destiny.

Shadrach, Meshach and Abednego: Chose to walk in God's ways.

Daniel 3 tells the story of three young men who made a decision to walk in the ways of God and would not yield to the pressures of their culture. Everyone around them was bowing to the idol. They could have gone along, but they would not. They chose to walk in the ways of God and it set their destiny.

They state their position in Daniel 3:17-18: "Our God whom we serve is able to deliver us from the burning fiery furnace, and He will deliver us from your hand, O king. But if not, let it be known to you, O king, that we do not serve your gods, nor will we worship the gold image which you have set up." They took a stand on their trust in God and would not waver and God honored that trust.

What path do you choose?

What is the decision that is laying in front of you today? What ways are you contemplating? Remember, the ways you choose determine your path and your path determines your destiny. The decisions you make form your lifestyle and your lifestyle directs you towards your destiny.

Choose to follow God with your whole heart. Choose to live an unshakable life. Choose to live this faith declaration.

Faith Declaration #6:
I Will Walk on a Level Path

I will choose a lifestyle of integrity and I will walk according to the principles of God's word. I will learn God's ways and walk on a level path.

I Will Not Lose Heart

I will resist the lies of the enemy that seek to blind my eyes to the goodness and greatness of God working in my life. My God is for me and is able to strengthen my heart at all times so I refuse to lose heart.

Psalm 27:13-14
"I would have lost heart, unless I had believed that I would see the goodness of the Lord In the land of the living. Wait on the Lord; Be of good courage, and He shall strengthen your heart; Wait, I say, on the Lord!"

Chapter 9

I Will Not Lose Heart

*I*n the 1968 Olympic games in Mexico, the runner from Tanzania, John Akhwari, fell and dislocated his knee. Officials tried to convince him to quit, but he refused. With his knee bandaged, Akhwari picked himself up and hobbled the remaining 7.5 miles to the finish line, entering the stadium an hour after the last runner had already finished the race. Even though most of the crowd had already left, he limped around the stadium and collapsed over the finish line. It is one of the most heroic efforts of Olympic history.

Afterward he was asked by a reporter why he had not dropped out when told to do so by the medical personnel, Akhwari said, "My country did not send me to start the race. They sent me to finish." Pain could not remove from his heart the attitude of a finisher. He refused to lose heart.

The resolves of our heart are what will keep us going during the dark days of discouragement and disappointments. Live your life with non-negotiables which you will not compromise under pressure, change under busyness or neglect under the routines of life. 1 Corinthians 15:58 says, "Therefore, my beloved brethren, be steadfast, immovable, always abounding in the work of the Lord, knowing that your labor is not in vain in the Lord."

Martin Luther the great, never-give-up reformer had a "I will not lose heart" about life and ministry declaring, "These are the articles on which I must stand, and, God willing, shall stand even to my death; and I do not know how to change or to yield anything in them."[1]

Whatever you do, don't lose heart. Don't stop. Don't give in. Hold your ground. A person of tenacity has backbone, resoluteness, determination, firmness, persistence, a fixed purpose of mind and a settled commitment.

Faith Declaration

David sets out His resolve to not lose heart in Psalm 27:13-14. "I would have lost heart, unless I had believed that I would see the goodness of the Lord in the land of the living. Wait on the Lord; Be of good courage, and He shall strengthen your heart; Wait, I say, on the Lord" (Psalm 27:13-14).

This scripture is the foundation for our seventh faith declaration. Declare today with tenacity, faith and enthusiasm:

I will resist the lies of the enemy that seek to blind my eyes to the goodness and greatness of God working in my life. My God is for me and is able to strengthen my heart at all times so I refuse to lose heart.

Hear the promise of God in Isaiah 41:10: "Don't be afraid, for I am with you. Do not be dismayed, for I am your God. I will strengthen you. I will help you. I will uphold you with my victorious right hand."(*New Living Translation*). Or as *The Message Bible* puts it, "Don't panic. I'm with you. There's no need to fear for I'm your God. I'll give you strength. I'll help you. I'll hold you steady, keep a firm grip on you." We have all the help we will ever need in and through the grace of God. Resolve to hold your faith perspective, seeing the best things in the worst of circumstances.

Katherine Bevis tells how among the students at a well-known college there was a young man who had to get about on crutches. He had an unusual talent for friendliness and optimism and so won the deep respect of his classmates. One day a student asked him what had caused his deformity. "Infantile paralysis," he replied briefly, not wishing to elaborate on his difficulties. "With a misfortune like that, how can you face the world so?" inquired his classmate. "The disease never touched my heart," replied the young Christian, smiling.

Galatians 6:9 says, "And let us not grow weary while doing good, for in due season we shall reap if we do not lose heart." Add to that an "always-get-up" attitude as stated in Micah 7:7-8, "Therefore I will look to the Lord; I will wait for the God of my salvation; My God will hear me. Do not rejoice over me, my enemy; When I fall, I will arise; When I sit in darkness, the Lord will be a light to me."

Guard Your Heart

Proverbs 4:23 is a well-known scripture that says, "Keep your heart with all diligence, for out of it spring the issues of life." Your heart is the important component in your life journey. Guard your core. Guard your resource. Guard your spiritual flow. Just as the physical heart is the key to a healthy long life, so the spiritual heart is the key to a healthy spiritual life.

Researchers have found "a critical link between the heart and brain. The heart is in a constant two-way dialogue with the brain — our emotions change the signals the brain sends to the heart and the heart responds in complex ways. However, we now know that the heart sends more information to the brain than the brain sends to the heart. And the brain responds to the heart in many important ways."[2]

When you begin to feel anger or another strong emotion, your heart changes its rhythm and sends signals to the brain which is negatively affected in its ability to process information. If your spiritual heart gives up, it affects your ability to face life and live strong.

Those Who Lose Heart

Those who lose heart are discouraged.

They are disheartened and depressed. Their spirit is broken and their heart is broken. In Job 7:14-16, Job cries out in despair, "Even when I try to forget my misery in sleep, you terrify me with nightmares. I would rather die of strangulation than go on and on like this. I hate my life. (The Living Bible)"

Martin Luther was one who lost heart through discouragement. At times he even doubted God's willingness or ability to help him through a difficult season of life. His wife tired of his bouts of depression so one morning she silently put on a black dress and veil, clothes normally worn for times of mourning. When Luther asked her why she was dressed in mourning, she replied, "Because God is dead. It's obvious by the way you're acting."[3]

Is your God dead or alive? If He's alive, then why live as if He were dead? Stand on the unshakable foundation of His Word and allow His Spirit to breathe life and strength back into you.

Those who lose heart are faint-hearted.

The faint-hearted are those who don't have the resources to be strong. Of the Israelites, the Psalmist said, "Hungry and thirsty, their soul fainted in them" (Psalm 107:5). Lack of nourishment, lack of provision, led to their lack of strength to continue.

Faint-hearted people lack the spiritual nourishment that provides strength in seasons of shaking. They lack the inner fortitude to bear up under extended periods of trials. The marathoner John Akhwari may have lacked the natural health to persevere, but he had an inner resource that provided the strength he needed to continue.

What are you lacking? Are you lacking strength? Are you lacking resolve? Are you lacking fortitude? Psalm 107 continues on, "Then they cried out to the Lord in their trouble, and He delivered them out of their distresses. . . .Oh, that men would give thanks to the Lord for His goodness, and for His wonderful works to the children of men! For He satisfies the longing soul, and fills the hungry soul with goodness" (Psalm 107:6,8-9). Cry out to the Lord and He will satisfy your soul with the inner resources to not lose heart.

Those who lose heart are oppressed.

The oppressed person is the one who is being dominated by someone with greater power. The oppressor exercises harsh control over them, pressing them down and crushing their spirit. They feel powerless. Acts 10:38 says, "God anointed Jesus of Nazareth with the Holy Spirit and with power, who went about doing good and healing all who were oppressed by the devil, for God was with Him." David rejoiced in Psalm 9:9, "The Lord also will be a refuge for the oppressed, a refuge in times of trouble." God will be a shelter, a place of hope and trust. He will be a refuge where they can flee when the storms come and find strength and protection.

Those who lose heart are distressed.

To be distressed is to be in a place of extreme affliction, to have the walls close in around and squeeze someone into a tight place. A person who is distressed is a person who has had his world fall down around him. A distressed person is the young mom with two toddlers who has just been told her husband was killed in a car accident. It is a young couple whose child has been diagnosed with terminal cancer.

Has your world fallen in on you? God's promise to the distressed person is Romans 8:35 and 37. "Who shall separate us from the love of Christ? Shall tribulation, or distress, or persecution, or famine, or nakedness, or peril, or sword? ... Yet in all these things we are more than conquerors through Him who loved us." You will conquer through Him. You will make it through in His love. Don't give up. He's with you.

Those who lose heart are weary.

Weary people have completely lost spirit; they are worn out and exhausted. They have run hard for a long time and reached the end of their strength. There is nothing left in them, no resources to pull from. It hasn't been a one-time earthquake, but it is an ongoing shaking as tremor after tremor continues. Weary people have sustained blow after blow and their strength is buckling. They have stood underneath continuous pressure that has slowly pushed them to their knees.

In 2003 Andrew Halsey attempted to row across the Pacific Ocean. Four months and 2,300 miles into his trip, he ran into adverse weather conditions and currents that resulted in his receiving the dubious award of rowing the longest time to go the shortest distance. For 72 days he rowed 31 miles a day and went nowhere. The currents pinned him in one place. That's enough to make anyone weary and ready to quit. 72 days of work. 72 days of going nowhere. Instead his response was, "You can't row across an ocean and the first time you get a bit of bad weather say let's quit."[4]

Perhaps you aren't rowing across the Pacific Ocean, but you are struggling against adverse circumstances. You have held up under challenge after challenge in raising your children, but live in fear that the next challenge will be too big for you to handle. You have stood firm and faith-filled through ongoing medical crises as your husband has faced one problem after another, but you don't have enough strength to keep going.

David promises that you will see the goodness of God in your life so hang in there. Don't give up. You will see His hand on your life for good. There is hope, not just for eternity, but for here and now.

Those who lose heart are attacked.

1 Peter 5:8-10 warns, "Be sober, be vigilant; because your adversary the devil walks about like a roaring lion, seeking whom he may devour. Resist him, steadfast in the faith, knowing that the same sufferings are experienced by your brotherhood in the world. But may the God of all grace, who called us to His eternal glory by Christ Jesus, after you have suffered a while, perfect, establish, strengthen, and settle you."

When ongoing attacks come, it is easy to give up. You've lost one battle and here comes another one. Why keep trying? Why not give up? Because your God is greater than the enemy and you will overcome and defeat him – if you keep getting up.

Those who lose heart are afflicted.

A person can be afflicted with sickness, emotional strain or physical limitations. The sickness can be sudden and life-threatening or chronic and life-limiting. Emotional strain can be relational, financial or work-related. Whatever the affliction that a person faces, it can wear a person down until he loses heart and quits fighting.

Ted Engstrom wrote:

> "Cripple him, and you have Sir Walter Scott. Bury him in the snows of Valley Forge, and you have George Washington. Raise him in abject poverty and you have an Abraham Lincoln. Subject him to bitter religious prejudice and you have a Disraeli. Strike him down with infantile paralysis and he becomes a Franklin

D. Roosevelt. Burn him so severely in a school-house fire that the doctors say he will never walk again, and you have a Glenn Cunning-ham, who set the world's record in 1934 for running a mile in four minutes and 6.7 seconds. Deafen a genius composer and you have a Ludwig van Beethoven. Have him or her born black in a society filled with racial discrimination, and you have a Booker T. Washington, a George Washington Carver, or a Martin Luther King, Jr. Make him the first child to survive a Nazi concentration camp, paralyze him from the waist down when he is four, and you have an incomparable concert violinist, Itzhak Perl-man. Call him a slow learner, 'retarded,' and write him off as ineducable, and you have an Albert Einstein. As one man summed it up: Life is 20% what happens to us and 80% how we respond to the events."[5]

Victor Frankl spent three years in Nazi concentration camps. He wrote of his time there, "We who lived in concentration camps can remember the men who walked through the huts comforting others, giving away their last piece of bread. They may have been few in number, but they offer sufficient proof that everything can be taken from a man but one thing: the last of the human freedoms—to choose one's attitude in any given set of circumstances, to choose one's own way."[6]

How are you going to respond in your afflictions? What choice are you going to make? Are you going to lose heart and give up? Or are you going to say with Paul, "When I am weak, then I am strong" (2 Corinthians 12:10).

Those who lose heart are bewildered.

A person who is bewildered is a person who is perplexed or confused. The word bewilder finds its roots in the meaning "to thoroughly lead astray or lure into the wilds." A bewildered person is one who is led astray by life contradictions. Stephen and Paul were both stoned, but Stephen died and Paul lived. Peter and Paul both went to preach the gospel; Peter was instantly transported but Paul was shipwrecked. James and Peter were both imprisoned; James was beheaded and Peter was released. Life doesn't make sense!

Why does a hardened criminal and murderer live to be an old man and a young child dies of cancer at the age of five? Why is a couple who desperately wants a child unable to conceive, while a teenager gets pregnant? Life doesn't make sense. It hurts and it doesn't make sense. So what do you do when your visions and dreams are fading away unfulfilled? How do you live with the pain of contradictions? How do you handle others having what you earnestly desire but they do not?

Remember David's assurance. Even when I walk through valleys, valleys that are deep and dark, valleys that stretch on with no end in sight. Even when I walk through valleys of loss, valleys of pain, valleys of terror. Even when life doesn't make sense, I will not fear because You are with me. I will not fear, because You are here (Psalm 23:4).

Your confidence is not in your ability to walk through valleys. Your confidence is not in your ability to see in the dark. Your confidence is in Him and in His hand holding you even when you can't see it or feel it. He's there. That is enough.

Those Whose Hearts are Strengthened

"Be of good courage and He will strengthen your heart!" (Psalm 27:14)

Lay hold of that promise! That is the word of God for you today. If you are discouraged, God will strengthen your heart. If you are distressed, He will push back the walls closing in around you. If you are weary, afflicted, or bewildered, He will provide the inner resources for you to stand strong.

God will strengthen your heart. He will make it strong and alert. He will give you courage to stand strong. He will put your feet on a solid foundation that will not be shaken. He will give you the power to be stronger and more effective. He will give you ongoing strength, not just a one-time strength boost. He will pour in a flood of His presence and His strength.

God strengthens those with stubborn determination.

Naomi was returning back to Israel so she said goodbye to her daughters-in-law. Orpah said her farewells and left, but Ruth refused to leave. Ruth 1:18 says, "When Naomi realized that Ruth was determined to go with her, she stopped urging her" (*NIV*). Ruth was determined. She had a strong determination that refused to give up. Her mind was set and she would not be swayed.

Andrew Jackson, the seventh president of the United States, was known as a stubborn man. When he was a boy, he frequently wrestled with another boy named Jim Brown, who won three times out of four. Why three out of four? Because Andrew would not give up. He was outclassed and outweighed by Jim, but he would wrestle and get thrown, wrestle and get thrown, over and over. But on the fourth match Jim would be tired. He would be slowing down and Andrew would win. What was the secret of his victory? Not talent. Not brute strength. Stubborn determination. He would never admit he was beat, but would get back up and go again.

Get the Ruth spirit in your spirit. God will put into you a stubborn determination that refuses to give up when life gets difficult. You will not quit when you are overwhelmed. You will not turn back when life doesn't make sense.

God strengthens those who trust without seeing.

It was a contradiction. It didn't make sense. King Ahaz had locked up the house of God, built altars to idols, worshipped idols and did everything he could to provoke God. Hezekiah stepped in as king and immediately began to reverse those things. He restored the temple, restored worship to the true God, reinstituted the Passover, brought the Word of God back into the lives of the people. He did everything he could to rule righteously.

The result? 2 Chronicles 32:1 records that "After these deeds of faithfulness, Sennacherib king of Assyria came and entered Judah; he encamped against the fortified cities, thinking to win them over to himself." After Hezekiah acted faithfully, after he set the nation to seek God, after he turned to righteousness, everything turned bad.

The natural way of thinking says God should bless and protect him because he was doing right. Attacks should come when the nation is living in wickedness. Instead 2 Chronicles says, "After these deeds of faithfulness," the enemy attacked.

Hezekiah's response to his troops is given in 2 Chronicles 32:7-8: "Be strong and courageous; do not be afraid nor dismayed before the king of Assyria, nor before all the multitude that is with him; for there are more with us than with him. With him is an arm of flesh; but with us is the Lord our God, to help us and to fight our battles."

He did not look at the natural things. He didn't look at the size of Sennacherib's army. He didn't consider the strength of the weapons aligned against him. He looked in the spiritual and saw the unseen. "There are more with us than with him." Sennarcherib had more armies. He had more men, more chariots and more horses. He had more swords and spears, more bows and arrows, but Hezekiah had the Lord God. He trusted what he could not see. He trusted in the Lord his God even in the face of overwhelming odds.

Strengthen Your Heart

Strengthen your heart by knowing your God.

If you have a faulty concept of who God is you will have a twisted faith that is governed by your emotions. You can make great faith declarations and speak positive words, but your faith and positive attitude will be based on your own emotions and feelings and not on God. That kind of faith will end in disillusionment.

Know your God. Know His nature and His character. Understand the sovereignty of God and the love of God. Learn to know your God intimately. A stage actor used to close his act each night by reciting the Twenty-third Psalm. He would eloquently quote the passage, with perfect inflection, his voice rising to majestic declarations and dropping to sacred whispers. When he finished, the crowd would always rise to their feet in thunderous applause. One day a quiet young man stood and requested permission to recite the psalm instead. The actor smiled as he graciously granted it. The young man could never surpass his own eloquency and skill, but would only make the actor himself appear that much better after his stumbling oratory.

The young man shyly came forward and stood in the center of the stage. In a quiet voice he began to quote the Psalm. "The Lord is my shepherd. I shall not want." Softly, without melodrama, he ended "And I shall live in the house of the Lord forever." The audience sat in captivated silence as tears flowed from every eye. The only sound was that of quiet weeping as the impact of those verses settled into each heart.

The actor approached the young man, "How did you do it? How did you move them to tears? How did you impact them so? I have studied this psalm for years and I know it better than anyone and I cannot do that. How can you do it?" The young man simply replied, "You know the psalm. I know the author."

Study the Word of God. Know it for it gives strength to our spirits. But unless you know the author, the true power of the words is lost. Know your God. Know Him.

Strengthen your heart by holding to your faith in God and His word.

"For the word of God is living and powerful, and sharper than any two-edged sword, piercing even to the division of soul and spirit, and of joints and marrow, and is a discerner of the thoughts and intents of the heart"(Hebrews 4:12).

Believe the Word of God. Believe God will do what He promised. Believing the Word of God means to stand firm on it and to trust it. If you believe it, it will change the way you live. It will change the way you act and think. Abraham believed God's word that he would be the father of many nations, but he had no children. He believed first and saw later (Genesis 15:6: "And he believed in the Lord; and He counted it to him for righteousness.")

Jehoshaphat believed that God would rescue them from the enemy and it changed his battle plan. Instead of going into battle with fear and trembling, he sent his army in worshipping and saw God deliver. 2 Chronicles 20:20-21 says, "'Hear me, O Judah and you inhabitants of Jerusalem: Believe in the Lord your God, and you shall be established; believe His prophets, and you shall prosper.' And when he had consulted with the people, he appointed those who should sing to the Lord, and who should praise the beauty of holiness, as they went out before the army and were saying: 'Praise the Lord, for His mercy endures forever.'"

Believe God is who He says He is. In Isaiah 43:10 God says of Himself, "'You are My witnesses,' says the Lord, 'And My servant whom I have chosen that you may know and believe Me, and understand that I am He. Before Me there was no God formed, nor shall there be after Me.'"

Strengthen your heart by seeing beyond the immediate into the eternal.

Open up your heart and see with faith-eyes what the natural man cannot see with the natural eyes. See God working in the dark. See God turning situations around. See God in every aspect of life.

Helen Keller had been blind since she was a child, yet she made the profound statement, "I can see, and that is why I can be happy in what you call the dark, but which to me is golden. I can see a God-made world, not a man-made world."[7]

2 Corinthians 4:16 says, "Therefore we do not lose heart. Even though our outward man is perishing, yet the inward man is being renewed day by day."

You don't lose heart because your eyes are not set on the temporal but on the eternal. Your eyes are set on the inward man, not the outward.

"We do not look at the things which are seen, but at the things which are not seen. For the things which are seen are temporary, but the things which are not seen are eternal" (2 Corinthians 4:18).

Eyes focused on what can be seen around you will cause you to lose heart because life is full of difficulties and unexplained trials. Eyes focused on God see past these things to why we were created, past these things to the things that are permanent. The trials of today are temporary. Even if they last an entire lifetime, they are temporary. In light of eternity, how long is 70 years?

In the days of Christopher Columbus, the Spanish motto was "non plus ultra," no more beyond. After Columbus discovered the new world, they built a monument in his honor. On the monument is the Spanish motto with a lion tearing away the first three letters so the motto now reads "plus ultra"—more beyond.

There is more beyond. Like the Spanish you can be limited by what you have heard, limited by what you see, and feel that there is nothing beyond this current trial. But lift your eyes and look beyond. Look to the eternal God and see with Paul, "For our light affliction, which is but for a moment, is working for us a far more exceeding and eternal weight of glory" (2 Corinthians 4:17).

2 Timothy 4:6-8 also tells of more beyond: "I have fought the good fight, I have finished the race, I have kept the faith. Finally, there is laid up for me the crown of righteousness, which the Lord, the righteous Judge, will give to me on that Day, and not to me only but also to all who have loved His appearing."

Strengthen your heart by trusting in the goodness of God.

Satan tries to get you to believe that God is holding back something good from you and that you would be better off if you turned away from Him to do as you pleased. He told Eve in Genesis 3:4-5, "You will not surely die. For God knows that in the day you eat of it your eyes will be opened, and you will be like God, knowing good and evil." He does the same thing today. "If God really loved you, He wouldn't allow these things to happen." "If God really loved you, He would let you have what you really want."

God's goodness is not God doing something nice for you to make you happy. God's goodness is an expression of His mercy. It goes beyond our own comprehension. Psalm 31:19 marvels, "Oh, how great is Your goodness, which You have laid up for those who fear You, which You have prepared for those who trust in You in the presence of the sons of men." How great and how marvelous. How far beyond our understanding.

When Moses asked to see God, God replied, "I will make all My goodness pass before you, and I will proclaim the name of the Lord before you. I will be gracious to whom I will be gracious, and I will have compassion on whom I will have compassion" (Exodus 33:19). The goodness of God is part of His nature. It is who He is.

Look at Exodus 34:5-7. Moses stood on the mountain of the Lord and the Lord came down and appeared before him. "Now the Lord descended in the cloud and stood with him there, and proclaimed the name of the Lord. And the Lord passed before him and proclaimed, 'The Lord, the Lord God, merciful and gracious, longsuffering, and abounding in goodness and truth, keeping mercy for thousands, forgiving iniquity and transgression and sin, by no means clearing the guilty, visiting the iniquity of the fathers upon the children and the children's children to the third and the fourth generation.'"

This is the goodness of the Lord that we will see in the land of the living. No matter what situation you are going through, no matter what trial you are facing, you will see the hand of God extended towards you in mercy and grace. He will not remove His lovingkindness from your life. He will not leave you to walk through the trials alone.

An old map of North America from 1525 is displayed in the British Museum in London. In the unexplored regions represented on the map, the cartographer had written in what he expected to be there: "Here be giants," "Here be fiery scorpions," and "Here be dragons." That is what the sailors expected to find as they explored the unknown that laid ahead and so they explored fearfully.

In the early 1800s a British explorer by the name of Sir John Franklin was given possession of the map. He crossed out the words of fear and boldly wrote, "Here is God."[8]

Stop looking at your life and seeing giants, scorpions and dragons. Stop looking at what lies ahead in fear. Speak to your heart now, "Here is God." Set your eyes on your God. Say with faith, "I would have despaired, I would have lost heart and given up, except that I knew I would not walk through these trials alone. I know His hand of mercy and grace will be upon my life and in Him I will find all I need to walk through this season."

Strengthen your heart by waiting on the Lord.

Just to reinforce how important this point is, David repeats it in Psalm 27:14. "Wait on the Lord; be of good courage, and He shall strengthen your heart; Wait, I say, on the Lord!" Wait has the idea of holding on strongly. During the time of holding on, to become wound together with the object of the waiting.

It is the picture of a rope. A rope is made by several strands of twine being twisted together until they form one unit, one piece of rope. The ropemaker stretches the strands firmly in his hand and begins to twist them individually until they are twisted into a thicker and tightly wound strand. He then puts all the strands together and twists those, always maintaining a firm hand and tension to keep them from falling apart. Even if you combined all the strands together in one group, they would never equal the strength of the rope after it has been bound together under great pressure.

There is a tension in waiting on God. It isn't a passive event. It is laying straight and firm in the hand of God and allowing Him to twist you, binding you closer to Him. As you do, your strength is magnified and increased for you are no longer trusting in your strength alone but in the strength of your life being tightly wound around God.

It isn't a loose binding that can easily be unraveled. A good rope is wound so tight that one strand cannot be easily separated from another. Like the strands of rope, you are tightly bound to God so that you cannot be separated from Him. You are waiting with steadfast endurance, allowing your situation to wrap you even more tightly into God, looking with eager expectation at what His hand is working in your life.

Waiting is expecting God to work. Isaiah 25:9 says, "Behold, this is our God; we have waited for Him, and He will save us. This is the Lord; we have waited for Him; we will be glad and rejoice in His salvation." It has a confidence and assurance that God is going to work, that He is going to reveal Himself, that He will accomplish His word.

Waiting is being patient and yielded. Waiting is patiently abiding in the Master's hand, knowing that the good that is in store is worth the perseverance to see it. It is yielded to Him, knowing that it is in God's power to grand or withhold and that its only hope is in Him. A person who waits on God is one who has faith and trust in Him at all times in all circumstances. In Psalm 130:5-6, David says, "I wait for the Lord, my soul waits, and in His word I do hope. My soul waits for the Lord more than those who watch for the morning—yes, more than those who watch for the morning."

Waiting is earnestly desiring God. It is yearning for Him with a confident expectation that He will show mercy and grace. Waiting is relying upon His faithfulness and being assured that the answer will come. Psalm 40:1 says, "I waited patiently for the Lord; and He inclined to me, and heard my cry."

Waiting renews your strength. Isaiah 40:31 reminds us, "Those who wait on the Lord shall renew their strength; they shall mount up with wings like eagles; they shall run and not be weary; they shall walk and not faint." Waiting exchanges your strength for God's strength. As you are tightly wound around Him, you are bound so close that the two become inseparable and His strength is your strength.

As the trials of life come, your strength can be diminished. Your heart can lose its energy and its confidence in God. It can become weak and fearful. In waiting it is renewed. In waiting your strength is exchanged for His strength. Waiting is recognizing that in Him is all that you need for the journey or the trial. It is seeing that the grace of God as available and sufficient for every need and every struggle. In waiting you do not lose heart.

Faith Declaration #7:
I Will Not Lose Heart

I will resist the lies of the enemy that seek to blind my eyes to the goodness and greatness of God working in my life. My God is for me and is able to strengthen my heart at all times so I refuse to lose heart.

Chapter 10

Embracing Your Future with Passion and Confidence

The seven faith declarations we have developed from Psalm 27:1-14 are trustworthy wisdom for all who seek to live a blessed and favored life. We have made a clear and significant decision to stand on the Word of God and by faith speak the biblical declarations which will propel our life into a blessed destiny.

Let us read with faith these seven unshakable life declarations from Psalm 27.

▶ *1. I Will Live Life Strong*

I will not faint or be feeble. I will have strength and power greater than average or what is expected. I will be able to stand firm, to sustain any and all attacks. I will endure because I am established and well-fortified in my God.

▶ *2. I Will Love God's House Passionately*

I will love God's house with a faithful and fervent spirit and a heart of unwavering devotion, service and zeal.

▶ *3. I Will Hold My Head High*

I will boldly declare the greatness of God and the power of His Word. I will not live in defeat, but will stand my ground and fearlessly praise my God. I know God will lift me up and I will live life with my head held high.

▶ *4. I Will Have an Overflowing Heart*

I will fill my heart with God's Word, prayer and praise. For out of my heart overflow, the inner voice of God is heard clearly, powerfully and distinctly.

▶ *5. I Will Turn to God at All Times*

I will turn my eyes toward God, who is always ready and willing to help me in any and all of my life situations, even when I don't believe, see or feel God.

▶ *6. I Will Walk on a Level Path*

I will choose a lifestyle of integrity and I will walk according to the principles of God's word. I will learn God's ways and walk on a level path.

▶ *7. I Will Not Lose Heart*

I will resist the lies of the enemy that seem to blind my eyes to the goodness and greatness of God working in my life. My God is for me and is able to strengthen my heart at all times so I refuse to lose heart.

With these seven declarations securely in your heart and by faith in your mouth, you can move into your future with passion and confidence. You are blessed and favored. Believe this and start living with passion the blessed life that God has already given you.

The Unshakable Life is a Blessed Life

The blessed life is a life of God's acceptance and approval on you. To be blessed is to know, feel and relish God's affirmation and assurance, acceptance and approval. It is the experience of being chosen, valued and enjoyed. Ephesians 1:3 says, "Blessed be the God and Father of our Lord Jesus Christ, who has blessed us with every spiritual blessing in the heavenly places in Christ."

We are marked for blessing and should open our heart and hands to receive all that God desires to pour into our lives. Numbers 6:24-26 says, "The Lord bless you and keep you; The Lord make His face shine upon you, and be gracious to you; The Lord lift up His countenance upon you, and give you peace."

The blessed life is a life of God's honor on you. God desires to honor you with a life that is highly regarded by God and others, a life highly respected and esteemed. 1 Chronicles 29:12 tells of God's honor: "Both riches and honor come from You, and You reign over all. In Your hand is power and might; In Your hand it is to make great and to give strength to all." (See also Proverbs 22:4; Isaiah 61:7; Psalm 71:21.)

The Psalmist encourages us with words that should inspire us to a new level of expectancy, "For the Lord God is a sun and shield; The Lord will give grace and glory; No good thing will He withhold from those who walk uprightly" (Psalm 84:11). You have already made this decision to walk with integrity, live by the seven declarations of Psalm 27, and live a blessed and favored life.

A person who is blessed is a person who:

➤ Makes right decisions and has deep roots

"**Blessed** is the man who walks not in the counsel of the ungodly, nor stands in the path of sinners, nor sits in the seat of the scornful; But his delight is in the law of the Lord, and in His law he meditates day and night. He shall be like a tree planted by the rivers of water, that brings forth its fruit in its season, whose leaf also shall not wither; and whatever he does shall prosper" (Psalm 1:1-3).

➤ Receives forgiveness daily

"**Blessed** is he whose transgression is forgiven, whose sin is covered. **Blessed** is the man to whom the Lord does not impute iniquity, and in whose spirit there is no deceit" (Psalm 32:1-2).

➤ Trusts at all times

"Oh, taste and see that the Lord is good; **Blessed** is the man who trusts in Him!" (Psalm 34:8)

"**Blessed** is that man who makes the Lord his trust, and does not respect the proud, nor such as turn aside to lies" (Psalm 40:4).

➤ Is merciful to the poor

"**Blessed** is he who considers the poor; The Lord will deliver him in time of trouble. The Lord will preserve him and keep him alive, and he will be **blessed** on the earth; You will not deliver him to the will of his enemies" (Psalm 41:1-2).

➤ Is chosen by God

"**Blessed** is the man You choose, and cause to approach You, that he may dwell in Your courts. We shall be satisfied with the goodness of Your house, of Your holy temple" (Psalm 65:4).

➤ Loves God's house

"**Blessed** are those who dwell in Your house; They will still be praising You. **Blessed** is the man whose strength is in You, whose heart is set on pilgrimage. ...O Lord of hosts, **blessed** is the man who trusts in You!" (Psalm 84:4-5,12)

➤ Has the heart of a learner

"**Blessed** is the man whom You instruct, O Lord, and teach out of Your law" (Psalm 94:12).

➤ Is upright and fair

"**Blessed** are those who keep justice, and he who does righteousness at all times!" (Psalm 106:3)

➤ Knows the place of resource

"**Blessed** is he who comes in the name of the Lord! We have **blessed** you from the house of the Lord" (Psalm 118:26).

➤ Walks in integrity

"**Blessed** are those who keep His testimonies, who seek Him with the whole heart!" (Psalm 119:1-2)

➤ Has a teachable spirit

"**Blessed** is the man who listens to me, watching daily at my gates, waiting at the posts of my doors" (Proverbs 8:34).

➤ Is generous on every occasion
"He who has a generous eye will be **blessed**, for he gives of his bread to the poor" (Proverbs 22:9).

"I will make you a great nation; I will **bless** you and make your name great; and you shall be a **blessing**" (Genesis 12:2).

➤ Is spiritually growing
"**Blessed** be the God and Father of our Lord Jesus Christ, who has blessed us with every spiritual blessing in the heavenly places in Christ" (Ephesians 1:3).

The Unshakable Life is a Favored Life

In the Hebrew the word favor means "to be pleased with, delight in, show bias toward, put your eye on so as to watch and bless continually." Favor goes beyond merely wishing success on someone to extending aid, counsel or effort to support them in their pursuit of success. When God takes delight in someone, He extends favor, setting His eye on them and watching out for them. He extends His infinite power, wisdom and might to bring them into a place of favor and blessing.

There's a story of a young man from Boston who applied for a job in a Chicago bank and was asked to send a letter of recommendation from his past employer. The investment house where he had previously worked in Boston was more than delighted and wrote a glowing letter in his behalf. His father, they wrote, was a Cabot; his mother was a Lowell. Further back was a happy blend of Saltonstalls, Peabodys, and other of Boston's first families. Several days later they received a second letter from the Chicago Bank asking for another letter of recommendation saying that the previous one was not sufficient for their purposes. "We are not contemplating using the young man for breeding purposes. Just for work."

Aren't you glad God's favor is not based on breeding! Proverbs 8:35 says, "For whoever finds me finds life, and obtains favor from the Lord." The favored life is one that receives special grace and kindness from God, a life that receives advantages for success. Favored!" Proverbs 12:2 says, "A good man obtains favor from the Lord." (See also Psalm 5:12; Psalm 30:4-5.) The favored life is a delightful life that has a high degree of godly pleasure and joy, full satisfaction and a sense of fulfillment.

Psalm 37:4 reads, "Delight yourself also in the Lord, and He shall give you the desires of your heart." And Psalm 36:7-8 tells more of the blessings of God: "How precious is Your lovingkindness, O God! Therefore the children of men put their trust under the shadow of Your wings. They are abundantly satisfied with the fullness of Your house, and You give them drink from the river of Your pleasures."

God desires you to be honored, favored, blessed, satisfied and prosperous. The seven declarations are simply a freeway we set our course on as we follow God all the days of our life.

The Unshakable Life is a Full Life

A full life is a path of life that overflows beyond all limitations. It is filled to the full extent with nothing lacking. God desires for you to life a full live, a life that is complete, satisfied and fulfilled. In contrast an empty life is never satisfied. Even when it has everything that should satisfy, it is unhappy and unfulfilled.

A full life is a life of good things. Psalm 16:11 says, "You will show me the path of life; In Your presence is fullness of joy; At Your right hand are pleasures forevermore." The Lord desires you to find fullness in life, fullness that comes from the right choices you make to live in and under the presence of God.

The Lord desires that you discover the pleasures He has created for you and has stored up for you. The word "pleasures" in Hebrew means to have those things which are lovely, pleasant, satisfying and lasting. The full life drinks from the rivers of God's pleasures. These rivers are flowing streams of delight, delicious streams, filled with the keys to living a full life, enjoying all of life – the storms and the peace, the mysteries and the answers – enjoying all that God has provided for our lives, now and the future.

The full life partakes of the pleasures of God and is "abundantly satisfied." A person who is abundantly satisfied is one who has drunk their fill and quenched their thirst completely. To live a full life you must drink in continually the good things of God. Psalm 36:8-9 says, "They are abundantly satisfied with the fullness of Your house, and You give them drink from the river of Your pleasures. For with You is the fountain of life; In Your light we see light." The full life person partakes of God and is saturated with His sufficiency.

The full life is satisfied with the fullness and abundance that God has provided in His house, His church, and His people. There is fullness of life to be enjoyed through the relationships, life principles and the wisdom for success in every area of life.

The full life is a reality to be reached, even by those who now have an empty or hungry soul. God will respond to the hungry heart, to the unresting soul. Those who are starving will respond by filling their lives with all His goodness. The starving soul can become the satisfied soul. Psalm 107:9 "For He satisfies the longing soul, and fills the hungry soul with goodness." In Jeremiah 31:25 God promises, "For I have satiated the weary soul, and I have replenished every sorrowful soul."

An Unshakable Life is a Life of More

God desires to speak clearly and specifically to you about the now and about your future. You are blessed, favored and you have committed yourself to live a life of faith. An unshakable life also hears and believes the thoughts God has for you about you. They are coming your way right now. God has thoughts toward you that will help you achieve what is in God's heart for you.

Jeremiah 29:11-12 says, "For I know the thoughts that I think toward you, says the Lord, thoughts of peace and not of evil, to give you a future and a hope. Then you will call upon Me and go and pray to Me, and I will listen to you." Psalms 85:8 reads, "I will hear what God the Lord will speak, for He will speak peace to His people and to His saints; but let them not turn back to folly." John 10:27 says, "My sheep hear My voice, and I know them, and they follow Me."

God desires to communicate with you. He is speaking. The problem is that people have become disoriented to His voice. God's voice, His gentle voice, comes our way through preaching, miracles, prayer, impressions on the heart, quickened scriptures, through other people or the Holy Spirit speaking to our heart. Listen. Believe. Act upon His words to you.

One word that is coming to you from God is the word "more." God desires that you live a full life, that you have more than enough, an overflow. More life, more joy, more satisfaction, more dreams, more faith, more new beginnings, more grace, more forgiveness, more answers to prayer, more possibilities, more of all God's great provisions.

More is great than what I expected and greater than what I needed. John 10:10 says, "The thief does not come except to steal, and to kill, and to destroy. I have come that they may have life, and that they may have it more abundantly." Notice the word "more" – more abundantly. More is a biblical word and a God-thought for you now.

Will you choose a life of more or less? Will you live a full life or an empty life? God's thoughts toward you are numerous with words of greatness, words of more, words of full and abundant. Psalms 40:5 reminds us that "Many, O Lord my God, are Your wonderful works which You have done; and Your thoughts toward us cannot be recounted to You in order; If I would declare and speak of them, they are more than can be numbered." Psalms 115:14 says, "May the Lord give you increase more and more, you and your children."

The seven declarations are principles that lead to a life of "more." Everyone desires more out of life yet not everyone has chosen the right path and principles to live by in order to see the "more" fulfilled. For the believer, the "more life" starts with a decision to choose Christ, but it certainly doesn't stop there. You must then choose the more principles that God has laid out in His word. Psalm 27:1-14 is a great place to dig in and believe God's word.

An Unshakable Life is a Life of Greatness

Times of shaking are times for God to show His greatness and to lift you into the greatness He has for your life. Many people desire great things in their life, but desire is not enough. You must live according to the principles and laws God has laid out in His word for achieving greatness.

Greatness in life is to experience the notable, remarkable and exceptional that God has stored up for you. There are great victories that lie ahead, a great work for you to accomplish, great abundance to flow through your hands and life and a great future designed specifically for you (Genesis 12:2; Exodus 11:3; Deuteronomy 3:24).

David, the writer of our seven declarations from Psalm 27, was blessed with greatness. 2 Samuel 5:10 says, "David went on and became great and the Lord God of hosts was with him." The same God that blessed David can and will bless you. You will be able to say with the Psalmist, "The Lord has done great things for us, and we are glad" (Psalms 126:3). Pray and believe that God desires to increase your greatness and to release His abundant blessings upon your life (Psalm 71:21; Ephesians 1:19).

A person of greatness is one who is considerably above average. They have distinguished themselves in their abilities, accomplishments or character. They have made unusual advancements, never settling for the status quo. Those who walk with faith through seasons of shaking will have the mark of greatness on their life.

An Unshakable Life is a Life of Faith

God can accomplish great things in your life as you live out the faith declarations we have set forth, but it takes faith to declare anything over your life from the word of God. Hebrews 11:1 says, "Now faith is the substance of things hoped for, the evidence of things not seen." Faith is the unquestioning confidence, the full persuasion, the unwavering trust that what God has said, He is able to do and will perform. Faith is the substance, the confidence, the substructure of things hoped for. It enables you to treat things hoped for as a property for which you already hold the deed. Faith is something that underlies visible conditions and guarantees a future possession. This means that things that have no reality in themselves are made real, given substance by faith.

Faith prays believing that you have already received them (Mark 11:24). It is not believing that God can, but that God will. Faith sees the invisible, believes the incredible and receives the impossible. It is the conviction of things not seen.

A faith declaration emerges from the Word of God.

A faith declaration is one that speaks the word of God daily and declares it to be the attitude and principles you will follow. You must go above your emotions, your reasoning, your own words and move into the realm of faith. Faith says, "I have it when I can't see it." Faith is the power to trust God, having the confidence that God will do what He says. Our trust and confidence for every day is in our God. With faith, declare these scriptures over your life:

Psalms 5:11
> But let all those rejoice who put their trust in You; Let them ever shout for joy, because You defend them; Let those also who love Your name be joyful in You.

Psalms 20:7
> Some trust in chariots, and some in horses; but we will remember the name of the Lord our God.

Psalms 56:3-4, 11
> Whenever I am afraid, I will trust in You. In God (I will praise His word), in God I have put my trust; I will not fear. What can flesh do to me? ... In God I have put my trust; I will not be afraid. What can man do to me?

Psalms 62:8
> Trust in Him at all times, you people; Pour out your heart before Him; God is a refuge for us.

Proverbs 3:5
> Trust in the Lord with all your heart, and lean not on your own understanding.

Proverbs 29:25

The fear of man brings a snare, but whoever trusts in the Lord shall be safe.

2 Corinthians 1:9

Yes, we had the sentence of death in ourselves, that we should not trust in ourselves but in God who raises the dead.

Confident faith speaks with the mouth what is in the heart, as Paul says in Romans 10:8, "But what does it say? 'The word is near you, in your mouth and in your heart.'"

Fill your mouth with these seven declarations and let them become your reality. Living faith is fed by the living word. As we feed on the living word, the power of the living spirit moves through our living heart and produces living action. Our faith becomes alive! 2 Corinthians 5:7 tells us, "For we walk by faith, not by sight."

As we grow in faith, we grow in our steps of faith. We grow in our actions of faith. We begin to see the promises of God working for us on a daily basis. 2 Thessalonians 1:3 reads, "We are bound to thank God always for you, brethren, as it is fitting, because your faith grows exceedingly, and the love of every one of you all abounds toward each other."

A.W. Tozer said, "To have faith we must immerse ourselves in the Scriptures. And faith must be exercised if it is to be effective. Faith, like a muscle, grows by stretching."[1]

We are people blessed and favored by God. We have been called to greatness, a life of faith and confidence in our God. If you do not expect to see any great things, you will not be disappointed for you will not see them. But those who expect them will see them. People of great faith with great unshakable faith declarations will do great things for God.

Endnotes

Chapter 1

1. Lee Strobel, *The Case for Faith* (Grand Rapids, MI: Zondervan Publishing House, 2000), p. 234.

2. Camey Van Rooy, "Beauty from Ashes," *Christian Quotation of the Day* (www.gospelcom.net, August 6, 2002).

Chapter 2

1. *U.S. News and World Report* (February 21, 1994), p. 67.

Chapter 4

1. Charles Colson, *The Body* (Dallas, TX: Word Publishing, 1992), p. 65

Chapter 5

1. Andrew Murray, *God's Best Secrets* (Grand Rapids, MI: Zondervan Publishing, 1975), p. 26.

2. ibid; p. 3.

3. Richard Nixon, quoted in *The Columbia World of Quotations* (New York: Columbia University Press, 1996), www.bartleby.com/66/. [25 November 2006.]

4. www.parentpresent.org. (http://www.parentpresent.org/inspiration.htm#k), 28 November 2006.

5. Andrew Murray, *God's Best Secrets* (Grand Rapids, MI: Zondervan Publishing, 1975), Dec 26.

Chapter 6

1. A.W. Tozer, *The Pursuit of God* (www.jesus.org.uk/vault/library/tozer_pursuit_of_god.pdf), 25 November, 2006.

2. Bible.org. (bible.org/illus/prayer), 25 November 2006.

3. Madame Guyon, *Experiencing God Through Prayer* (New Kensington, PA: Whitaker House, 1984).

4. C.S. Lewis, *Mere Christianity* (www.worldinvisible.com), http://www.mit.edu/~mcguyton/ABSK/MereChristianity/merech30.htm.

5. Andrew Murray, *God's Best Secrets* (Grand Rapids, MI: Zondervan Publishing, 1975), January 4.

Chapter 7

1. "Luther's Tabletalk" (http://www.sermonillustrations.com/a-z/p/prayer.htm), 29 November 2006.

2. F.B. Meyer, *Great Verses Through the Bible* (Grand Rapids MI: Zondervan Publishing 1966), p. 377.

Chapter 8

1. William Barclay, *Letters to the Galatians and Ephesians* (Westminster John Knox Press, 1976), p. 100.

2. Brother Lawrence, "The Closer Walk" (www.practicegodspresence.com/booklets/the_closer_walk.html).

3. F.B. Meyer, *The Secret of Guidance* (http://worldinvisible.com/library/fbmeyer/contents.htm), 29 November 2006.

Chapter 9

1. F. Bente and W.H.T. Dau, translators, "The Smalcald Articles: Articles of Christian Doctrine," *Triglot Concordia: The Symbolical Books of the Evangelical Lutheran Church* (St. Louis: Concordia Publishing House, 1921), pp. 453-529.

2. "Does Your Heart Sense Your Emotional State?" MSNBC.Com (www.msnbc.msn.com/id/11023208/from/ET/), 3 December 2006.

3. Unpublished class notes from Dr. John Hannah, Church History 201, Dallas Theological Seminary, 1976. (www.sermons.org/illustrations.html).

4. "100 Days Adrift," BBC.com (www.bbc.co.uk/ouch/news/btn/solorower.shtml), 5 March 2003.

5. Ted Engstrom, *The Pursuit of Excellence* (Grand Rapids, MI: Zondervan Publishing, 1982).

6. Ted Engstrom, *Motivation to Last a Lifetime* (Grand Rapids, MI: Zondervan Publishing, 1984), p 11-12.

7. Helen Keller, quoted in *The Columbia World of Quotations* (New York: Columbia University Press, 1996), www.bartleby.com/63/. [25 November 2006].

8. www.bible.org/illus/f/f-75.

Chapter 10

1. A.W. Tozer, "Growing Faith and Increasing Capacity," *Christians Unite* (articles.christiansunite.com/article5146.shtml), 4 December 2006.

IMAGINE

*Believe in the
Power of a Dream*

In this book, author Frank Damazio challenges you to rise above the limitations you place on yourself and to pursue the dream God has put in your heart. Begin with a foundation of faith—"the substance of things hoped for"—and then lift up your eyes to imagine and grasp God's desire for your future. Learn the steps to living life with vision and perseverance.

Hardcover, 4 3/4" x 6 1/2", 128 pages
978-1-59383-037-3
1-59383-037-8

PHONE 1.800.777.6057 • **WEB** www.CityChristianPublishing.com

BAGGAGE

Leaving Your Past Behind

Many of us get weighed down with baggage full of old memories, regrets, and hurts that we drag with us through the years. This baggage keeps us from reaching our goals, obstructs our relationships, and trips us up when we try to move forward. In this book, you'll learn to identify what's in your bag, then discover how to let it go and experience the freedom of God's grace.

Hardcover, 4 3/4" x 6 1/2", 128 pages
978-1-59383-038-0
1-59383-038-6

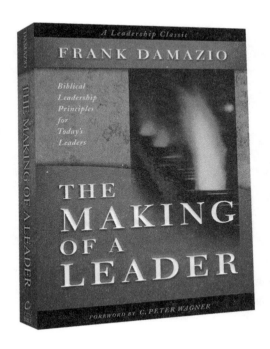

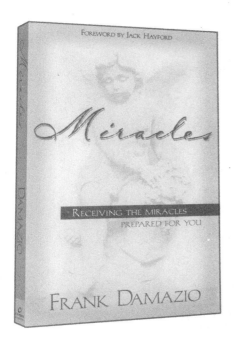

THE POWER OF SPIRITUAL ALIGNMENT

Living According to the Seven Firsts of Jesus

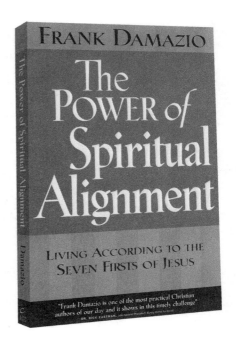

In a masterwork inspired by seven of Christ's priorities found in Matthew's gospel, Frank Damazio exposits the Scriptures and shows readers how to become more like Jesus and fulfill God's purpose for their lives. Learn to go from simply surviving to a victorious living that hits God's mark of destiny.

Softcover, 6" X 9", 174 pages
1-886849-87-0

PHONE 1.800.777.6057 • **WEB** www.CityChristianPublishing.com

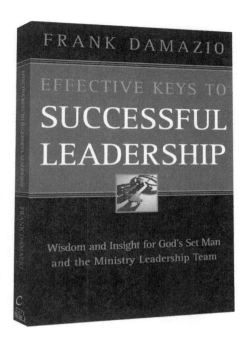

EFFECTIVE KEYS TO SUCCESSFUL LEADERSHIP

Wisdom and Insight for God's Set Man and the Ministry Leadership Team

Learn from this dynamic model what it takes to build an effective leadership team and a healthy local church. Common ministry temptations and tensions are candidly discussed, emphasizing the need for personal vision and mission in your ministry.

Softcover, 5 1/2" X 8 1/2", 225 pages
0-914936-54-9

FAX 503-257-2228 • EMAIL order@CityChristianPublishing.com

THE VANGUARD LEADER

Becoming a Strategic Leader

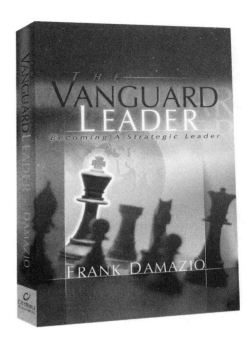

Author Frank Damazio defines the characteristics, function and motivation of vanguard leadership and encourages leaders everywhere to break free from the stagnation, mediocrity and complacency of the past. God's eternal purpose will be accomplished by a church that is prepared to face the unprecedented challenge and change of this era. *The Vanguard Leader* sets a bold new standard and charts a clear course for those navigating the troubled waters of the twenty-first century.

Softcover, 5½" X 8½", 330 pages
0-914936-53-0

PHONE 1.800.777.6057 • **WEB** www.CityChristianPublishing.com

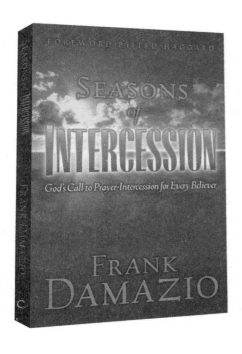